PROFESSIONAL SPEECH WRITING

by

DR. JERRY TARVER

THE EFFECTIVE SPEECH WRITING INSTITUTE
Richmond, Virginia

Published by
THE EFFECTIVE SPEECH WRITING INSTITUTE. .
P.O. Box 444
UNIVERSITY OF RICHMOND, VA 23173

Printed in the U.S.A. by
E. O. PAINTER PRINTING COMPANY
DELEON SPRINGS, FL 32028

Library of Congress Cataloging in Publication Data
TARVER, JERRY
   Professional speech writing
     1. Oratory. 2. Ghostwriting. I. Title.
PN4142.T37 1982   808'.066808   82-13813
ISBN 0-9609120-0-2

FIRST PRINTING

TABLE OF CONTENTS

To the participants
in my seminars,
who taught me more
than I taught them.

"Then the conclusion is obvious, that there is nothing shameful in the mere writing of speeches. But in speaking and writing shamefully and badly, instead of as one should, that is where the shame comes in."
Socrates, in Plato's *Phaedrus*

INTRODUCTION

"If speech writing can become an acquired art, with art's objective of reducing form and substance to their simplest and most effective terms, our people will rise up as a body in greatful appreciation." [Freshley, p. 105]

After several years of working with hundreds of speech writers, I have concluded that the typical speech writer is asked to do too much, in too short a time, with too little guidance. Exceptions exist, of course, but far too many writers are thrown into troubled seas and told to sink or swim.

I have written this book in the hope it will be of practical value to the working speech writer. I have two specific objectives in mind. One is to explain the basic principles of speech writing. I will attempt to describe systematically the techniques that make speech writing an "art" that can be acquired. For the experienced writer who examines this book, the explanation will take the form of a review, an opportunity to rethink the principles on which successful practice is based. For the less experienced writer, I hope the techniques will offer practical guidance to getting the next speech written competently and confidently.

My second objective is to discuss speech writing as a profession. I think speech writers need to be fully aware of the tradition behind their work. They need to be concerned about the status of speech writing and the problems speech writers face. Because speech writers often have little contact with others engaged in the same profession, they may not realize that many of the difficulties they struggle to overcome are also encountered by large numbers of their fellow writers. I hope the material on professional issues will be regarded as practical rather than merely incidental. I believe the quality of a writer's work depends in part on the writer's sense of self-worth and the writer's pride in belonging to a profession of importance.

Parts of this book are directed specifically to meeting the first objective. For example, chapters on content, structure, and language provide useful writing techniques. Parts of the book primarily support the second objective. For instance, the chapter

1

on the history and status of the speech writer presents information of professional interest. Some material in the book supports both objectives. The discussion of the working relationship between the speaker and the writer deals in equal measure with techniques for writing better speeches and with matters of professional conduct.

Anyone interested in studying speech writing in more depth than presented here will find a helpful guide in the bibliography at the end of the book. The bibliography includes, but is not limited to, sources of all material quoted in these pages. In order to avoid cumbersome footnotes, sources of quotations are simply indicated in brackets and give the author's last name and the page number of the citation.

If you have picked up this book as a first-aid kit for a speech you are already working on, a glance at the chapter titles will suggest which topics should be taken up immediately and which should be deferred. You might want to skim through Chapter II on working with your speaker to see if you find any useful advice. Then read consecutively Chapter III on audience, Chapter IV on structure, Chapter V on content, and Chapter VI on language. You can next decide if you need to scan Chapter VII on humor or Chapter VIII on delivery. After you complete your writing assignment you can return to Chapter I on the history and status of the speech writer and to Chapter X on speech in the communication program.

Before turning to professional concerns and writing technique, two preliminary questions deserve consideration.

WHY READ A SPEECH?

Powerful arguments can be made against the effectiveness of manuscript speaking. A speaker's contact with an audience suffers when a speech is read. The need to follow the manuscript limits the speaker's ability to look at listeners, and if the speaker does look, little can be done to adapt to any reactions which might be observed. Speakers who depart from their texts in order to adjust to audience response usually find it difficult to make a smooth return to their prepared remarks. Also, most speakers do not read well. Their voices tend to be monotonous and artificial. Emphasis can easily be misplaced, and often it appears to an audience that a speaker reading a manuscript doesn't have a firm grasp of the ideas being presented.

There exists a longstanding belief in our society that spontaneous remarks are somehow more trustworthy than a "calculated" statement. Common sense does not support this prejudice since we all know of cases where a lie was blurted out under pressure when the truth would have been told if time had allowed the preparation of a position paper. And certainly we recognize that "facts" presented on the spur of the moment do not have the probable accuracy of information carefully researched for a manuscript speech. But there remains, however unjustified it may be, what R. C. Jebb has called the "habitual presumption" that "speech is extemporary." [Jebb, Vol. I, pp. lxxi-lxxii.]

Consider these objections in the light of the time and expense involved in manuscript preparation, and we are fully entitled to ask, "why read a speech?" Some thoughtful answers can be offered to the question.

In the first place, speeches do not have to be read poorly. President Reagan may be considered one of the better examples of a speaker who can handle a manuscript well. An executive who does not have the time to research and organize a speech well enough to give it from notes may have the time to both collaborate on the writing and learn the material thoroughly enough to speak it intelligently. As will be pointed out in more detail in Chapter VIII, the speech writer may become a speech coach. Far too many speech writers have suffered from seeing their speeches "murdered" by an ill-prepared speaker. The job of the speech writer could justifiably extend to seeing the speech through to the moment of delivery.

Furthermore, good delivery is a relative matter. Perhaps a speaker who falls short of being an accomplished presenter of manuscripts would fare even worse in speaking extemporaneously. The manuscript might just be the lesser of the evils.

A second justification for manuscript speaking may be found in the advantages of precise wording this form of speaking permits. The manuscript allows careful advance study of language. Nuances of meaning can be considered, and ideas sharply defined. When George Romney stated in a press conference that he had been "brainwashed," his careless choice of words seriously damaged his political career. He would have been much better off with a prepared statement.

Harry Emerson Fosdick, a firm believer in writing sermons out in full, warned of some dangers of preaching without first committing words to paper: "monotonous style, a limited vocabulary with few synonyms, [and] repetitious ruts of thought." According to Fosdick, "Writing forces careful consideration of phraseology; makes the preacher weigh his words; compels him to reread what he has written and criticize it without mercy; constrains him to clear up obscurities in thought and language; begets discontent with repetitious mannerisms; and allows the preacher, before he mounts the pulpit, to listen, as it were, to his own sermon as a whole. . . ." [McGlon, p. 51]

The matter of precision extends to the time limit. Most audiences quickly lose interest in a speech that goes overtime. A speaker talking off the cuff may easily go past the time limit or may use up the allotted time on only half of the material that should have been covered. Writers who know their speaker's typical speaking rate can easily guarantee that the speech will end on time.

Some good speakers may choose not to read the manuscript and instead they may use it as the basis for a successful speech from notes. Such speakers will often follow the writer's pattern of ideas, they will depend on the writer's research for their evidence, and they will occasionally pick up key phrases from the written speech. John F. Kennedy followed this practice in his political campaigns. He departed so often from the manuscripts released to the press that reporters joked he was a "text deviate."

WHAT ARE THE ETHICAL CONSIDERATIONS?

Professor Ernest Bormann has compared the practice of speech writing to cheating on an exam or rigging a quiz show. Arguing that "deception is inherent" in speech writing, Bormann accepts the idea that a speaker can legitimately be helped in preparing a speech, but he insists that "at some point on the continuum of collaboration the place is reached where the speech changes character." [Bormann, pp. 263, 266-67] At that point Bormann insists speech writing has become unethical.

As Professor Donald Smith points out in a rebuttal, Bormann's comparison of speech writing with cheating on a test is not logical. A student, after all, is supposed to be learning and few observers would assume that to be the purpose of a business executive or political figure in giving a speech. [Smith, p. 417]

But Bormann does raise issues that need to be considered. Does the writing of a speech involve deception? And if so, would this make it unethical?

Smith argues that the presence of speech writers is well known and thus there is no deception. He states it would require "an aggressive level of ignorance" for a citizen of the United States not to know that the President has a staff of speech writers.

There is no denying, however, that the work of the speech writer is treated, if not "deceptively," then at least "discretely." As critics point out, the effectiveness of most speeches would be hampered by an announcement at the end stating "I wish to close with an expression of appreciation to my speech writer." But lack of acknowledgment does not make speech writing unethical. There are many things we would not do in public that we do in private, but that doesn't mean these behaviors are unethical. The critics of speech writing need to find stronger ground than secrecy on which to base their attack.

If the "deception" in speech writing extends to distorting public perception of the speaker, then a more substantial issue has been raised. Is a speech writer engaged in an unethical practice by making a speaker appear more intelligent, more articulate, or more witty than the speaker would be if the speaker had had the time to prepare the speech?

A political figure or a business leader can surely be permitted, or even encouraged, to draw on the best advice available. A president of the United States, for example, may well advocate a foreign policy or an economic program based on the ideas of others. We judge the quality of the president's mind and character by the worth of the synthesis we find in the final product. We would hardly call a presidential speech distorted simply because the president failed to credit each advisor for the part that advisor played in arriving at the policy. Nor would we insist that credit be given for every argument a president uses in defending a program under attack.

The question then becomes, must any speaker entitled to use advisors for ideas and arguments be compelled to phrase those ideas and arguments with no help? Obviously not. It would be absurd to say that the president of a corporation with no expertise in engineering can ethically adopt a recommended design for a new product and then not be allowed any aid in describing the product in a speech to the company's stockholders. In either deciding or explaining, no one assumes the president to be operating in a vacuum.

As the alter ego of the speaker, the writer too can borrow ideas and language from experts. As will be discussed in a later chapter, the writer must develop a network of advisors and must rely extensively in many cases on data supplied by others.

Only two restrictions should apply to the help speakers and writers receive. The discussion of speech writing in this book is based on the assumption that the practice is ethical *if the speaker and the writer (1) understand and (2) believe the material in the speech.*

In the case of an important speech in which the speaker is heavily involved in the preparation of the message, the speaker will routinely understand and believe what the speech says. In minor speeches, such as speeches of welcome or a speech presenting an award, a quick glance at the manuscript the day before delivery may be quite enough to guarantee that the speaker grasps and accepts the ideas.

Merely knowing and believing what is in the speech does not mean the speaker could have expressed the idea as well as the speech writer did. Taking one of Professor Bormann's concerns, what would be the ethical considerations in having the speech writer make the speaker sound witty if in fact the speaker is not? First of all, this "ethical dilemma" is not nearly as likely to occur as the professor might imagine. Making silk purses out of the ears of sows is as difficult as it ever was; an unwitty speaker is not going to turn into a comedy genius in the hands of some clever speech writer. But if a writer does *improve* the level of a speaker's humor, where is the ethical violation? Most people who are witty steal at least some of their material.

Who would claim that repeating a joke from *Reader's Digest* would be unethical just because a person failed to cite the source?

The same analysis can be applied to the writer who makes a dull speaker somewhat more interesting, a verbose speaker a bit more concise, or a rambling speaker better organized. Speech writers work from the same premise as Professor Bormann and the rest of the speech teachers in the field of education: a poor speaker can be improved. If a speaker did not manage to learn the effective use of language or methods of organization, a speech writer supplies the missing skill in the same way the accountants, lawyers, and engineers supply a business or political figure with ideas or procedures the speaker might not have learned in school. Of course, some busy speakers could, if they had the time, write their own speeches as well or better than a speech writer.

The ethical rule of "understanding and believing" will sometimes be violated. A writer may prepare a glowing tribute to a retiring executive who was strongly disliked by the writer and the speaker. A corporate executive may deliver a speech in support of a company policy the executive fought bitterly against while it was being decided. In short, writers and speakers will occasionally tell the same sorts of "white lies" most of us resort to when we say "you're looking well" to a friend who is ill but needs cheering up.

The speech writer's ethical problem, then, does not come about because of the nature of speech writing. It comes about because of the very nature of speech writing with all its opportunities for misrepresentation. The truly serious ethical questions come in asking, "Is this information accurate? If this position logical? Is this program in the best interest of the audience?" And these are questions that have nothing to do with who wrote the speech.

A writer—or a speaker—who invents or distorts a quotation is lying. A writer or a speaker who knowingly defends a position not supported by the evidence is deceiving. A writer or a speaker who distorts statistics, twists facts, or in any way "makes the worse appear the better cause" is behaving in an unethical manner.

Almost any issue a speech addresses has two sides. What is

"right" may be relative. Two honest and intelligent people may disagree strongly about what is true or correct. Speakers and speech writers have the ethical responsibility to tell the truth as they see it.

It should be noted that many professional speech writers do not accept the concept of ethics described here. They insist they have no ethical obligation to believe in the ideas they include in a speech. Regarding their work as that of the paid advocate, they—like lawyers—will sometimes defend a client or a cause they do not necessarily think is right.

CONCLUSION

Speech writing is a challenging task. It is both craft and art. Its techniques may be learned, but it often depends on the talent and sensitivity of the individual writer for its success.

CHAPTER I

HISTORY AND STATUS OF SPEECH WRITING

*"Those [in the fifth century B.C.] who had no leisure or
taste to become rhetoricians now began to find it worth
while to buy their rhetoric ready made."* [Jebb, Vol. I, p. 3]

Many people think speech writing developed as an outgrowth
of modern public relations. But the fact of the matter is
that professional speech writers have been around for centuries.

No one knows for sure who first prepared a speech for pay.
Maybe an early cave dweller, after winning community leadership by brute strength, found it necessary to purchase a few well
spaced grunts to utter at the big feast celebrating the success
of the autumn pig hunt. Or perhaps some ancient pharaoh hired
a grand vizier to write state speeches and compose royal prayers
to the sun god.

The Bible documents one remarkable early case. When the
Lord instructed Moses to tell the people of Israel to leave Egypt,
Moses declined with the excuse, "I am not eloquent . . . but I
am slow of speech, and of a slow tongue." As the story develops
in Chapter Four of the Book of Exodus, the Lord finally lost
patience with Moses and chose Aaron to deliver the message
with the explanation, "I know that he can speak well." But Moses
was made Aaron's speech writer when he was told "thou shalt
speak unto him, and put words in his mouth."

THE SPEECH WRITER IN CLASSICAL GREECE

By the time Greek civilization was flourishing near the end
of the fifth century B.C., speech writers were operating as a
recognized profession in the city of Athens. Among the more
famous of the speech writers, or "logographers," to use the Greek
term, was none other than Demosthenes. In addition to being the
most eloquent orator of his day, Demosthenes won recognition
in his early years as a prolific and highly paid writer of speeches
for others.

The most famous teacher of speech in ancient Greece was Isocrates. He competed for pupils with Aristotle and Plato, and at the start of his career was known to have composed speeches for pay. Another speech writer of classical times, Aspasia, helped Pericles write his speeches. She is reputed to have given advice on the best known of the addresses of Pericles, his eloquent Funeral Oration. Aspasia is cited in some literature as the "consort" of Pericles and is believed to have performed, in addition to her speech writing duties, certain additional services of a somewhat more personal nature.

One popular logographer of the fifth century B.C., Lysias, recouped a family fortune with the large fees he was able to command for his skill in speech writing. R. C. Jebb gives an account of Lysias' remarkable ability to vary his writing style:

> Although on a few occasions he himself came forward as a speaker, the business of his life was to write for others. All sorts of men were among his clients: all kinds of causes in turn occupied him. . . . If he had been content to adopt the standard which he found existing in his profession, he would have written in nearly the same style for all these various ages and conditions. He would have treated all these different cases upon a uniform technical system, merely seeking, in every case alike, to obtain the most powerful effect and the highest degree of ornament by applying certain fixed rules. Lysias was a discoverer when he perceived that a purveyor of words for others, if he would serve his customers in the best way, must give the words the air of being their own. He saw that the monotonous intensity of the fashionable rhetoric—often ludicrously unsuited to the mouth into which it was put—was fatal to real impressiveness; and, instead of lending to all speakers the same false brilliancy, he determined to give to each the vigour of nature. It was the desire of treating appropriately every case entrusted to him, and of making each client speak as an intelligent person, without professional aid, might be expected to speak under such circumstances, which chiefly determined the style of Lysias. [Jebb, Vol. I, pp. 159-160]

SIGNIFICANCE OF SPEECH WRITING

The Greek period in the history of speech writing offers three interesting insights into the logographer's art.

First, speech writing filled an important need. Greek law did not allow for the hiring of lawyers. Thus citizens who had to go before the courts, either to defend themselves or to bring charges against someone else, had to state their own cases. No law, however, forbade the purchase of a prepared address to be memorized and recited. The writers of the speeches were sometimes called on to offer advice on legal strategy and may have even helped their clients rehearse their speeches. In spite of the importance of speech writing, the logographers were not always highly regarded by society. They did not, for example, have the status of the sophists, the teachers who taught students to prepare and deliver their own speeches. Both Isocrates and Demosthenes appear to have been somewhat embarrassed by their labors as logographers. Both groups, teachers and writers, were well paid for their efforts. Whatever social stigma might have been attached to speech writing, the demand for the writers' services remained high.

Although speech writers did not attract the favorable attention the Greeks gave to the teachers of rhetoric, the writers used the techniques taught in the schools. So, the second lesson to be learned from a look at the classical logographers is that then, as now, speech writers possessed valuable technical knowledge about the process of communication. Without denigrating the natural talent so useful in either preparing or delivering a speech, it can be seen from the Greek experience that the techniques of speech preparation found in such books as Aristotle's *Rhetoric* could be put to practical use. The writers learned how to discover convincing arguments, how to organize them clearly, and how to express them in appropriate language.

Of course, any Greek citizen with the time and money could have enrolled in one of the schools to learn how to speak. The sophists traveled from city to city offering their instruction in rhetoric and other subjects. Even though Plato attacked rhetoric heatedly in some of his earlier dialogues, Aristotle finally brought the teaching of rhetoric into the Platonic Academy. The coexistence of the schools of rhetoric with the practice of speech writing brings us to the third conclusion to be drawn from the success of the logographers: they demonstrated the value of specialization. Learning to write a good speech could take years of study and experience. Those who chose to put their energies into other pursuits could turn to an expert on those occasions when help was needed.

DECLINE OF THE ART

Speech writing declined in importance as the Athenian democracy passed and the Roman dictatorship became the seat of power. Some have argued that the art of speech making, and one might assume the art of speech writing as well, thrives in a democracy but not when freedom is absent. Perhaps a better explanation for the change that occurred with the growth of Roman power was the increasing importance of the Roman lawyer. Roman society witnessed a bonding of skills in law, speech, and politics that was to reoccur throughout history.

Speech writing was not totally absent in Rome, but the only speech writers of note were on the payroll of the emperors. When Nero took power at the death of Claudius, he delivered a funeral oration written by Seneca. Seneca also supplied later material for Nero. Another emperor, Otho, employed Trachalus to aid in the preparation of his speeches.

PRESIDENTIAL SPEECH WRITERS

Other cases of speech writing might be cited from ancient history, but after the classical Greek period the next most important chapter in the history of speech writers is found in the story of the presidency of the United States. Although today's role for the White House speech writer was not created until the election of Franklin D. Roosevelt, several early presidents used the services of others in preparing speeches and public papers.

The first was George Washington. When it was discovered after Washington's death that he had been helped extensively by Alexander Hamilton in writing his Farewell Address, this startling information was kept secret for fifty years. At last the whole story came out, and it was revealed that a first draft of the address was written, at Washington's request, by James Madison. That draft was composed near the end of Washington's first term before he decided to serve another four years. As his second term drew to a close, Washington rewrote the Madison document and sent it to Hamilton who constructed an entirely new speech.

Washington edited the Hamilton version extensively for

style, but kept most of the ideas and much of the language. One of Hamilton's chief contributions was to remove a tone of petulance an angry Washington had at first included. Although the address was never actually delivered, it found its way to the public through newspaper publication and became one of the most famous documents in United States history. Much of the credit should go to a writer whose contribution was unknown until many years after his death.

President Andrew Johnson, whose wife taught him to read and write, found it useful to employ writers in the preparation of some of his veto messages and speeches. Johnson's habit of making rash and belligerent remarks when speaking off the cuff suggests he should have used speech writers more often.

Even Abraham Lincoln sought advice in preparing a major speech. When he began to write his first inaugural address he turned to several important speakers and political leaders. William H. Seward proposed some thirty-six changes in Lincoln's draft. These changes included two passages to replace the original ending of the speech. Lincoln discarded one of Seward's passages but chose to revise and retain the other. The revision shows Lincoln's openness to assistance as well as his speaking skill in his desperate attempt to calm a divided nation on the eve of a civil war:

Seward's Draft	Lincoln's Revision
I close. We are not, we must not be, aliens or enemies, but fellow-country and brethren. Although passion has strained our bond of affection too hardly, they must not, I am sure they will not, be broken. The mystic cords which, proceeding from so many battlefields and so many patriot graves, pass through all the hearths in this broad continent of ours, will yet harmonize in their ancient music when breathed upon by the guardian angel of the nation.	I am loath to close. We are not enemies, but friends. We must not be enemies. Though passion may have strained, it must not break our bonds of affection. The mystic chords of memory, stretching from every battlefield, and patriot grave, to every living heart and hearthstone, all over this broad land, will yet swell the chorus of the Union, when again touched, as surely they will be, by the better angels of our nature.

The assistance given to nineteenth century presidents of the

United States in the preparation of their speeches does not, of course, compare in extent or method to modern practices. In the examples cited above, advice was not sought in a systematic way, and advisors were orators and politicians rather than professional writers. The informality of the process may be seen in the story of Daniel Webster helping President Polk prepare his inaugural address. Much of Webster's valuable advice was rejected. About all he was able to do was to persuade the president to eliminate some of his dull and obscure classical references. As Webster told his friends, he had been successful only in killing off a few Roman centurions in the speech.

INFLUENCE OF WHITE HOUSE WRITERS

The cases of Washington, Jackson, Polk, and Lincoln are presented merely to confirm the fact that speech writing in America has a precedent reaching back before the start of the twentieth century. Speech writing in the White House is of interest, however, for another reason. Modern presidential speech writers are responsible to some degree for the importance of speech writing today both in government and in business. And their influence on speech writing extends beyond the boundaries of the United States.

The chief effect of presidential writers has been to bring speech writing out into the open. White House speech writers have not been noteworthy for either their modesty or their silence. Many of them, in violation of the code of anonymity that usually prevails, have made their contributions known to the public. In memoirs and magazine articles, White House speech writers have given us inside accounts of the practice of their art at the highest political level. They have thus contributed to the legitimization of the speech writing process. Lesser political figures as well as corporate executives are able to say, "If it's good enough for the president of the United States, it's good enough for me."

The impact of presidential speech writers on the profession does not stem merely from the rarefied status that comes from occupying the Executive Office Building in Washington. Speeches have been of crucial importance in the leadership of modern U. S. presidents, and public knowledge of the involvement of speech writers in major addresses has made clear the value of speech writing for speakers who desire to be effective.

An example of the extent to which presidential speech writers are in the public eye can be found in a lengthy article on Richard Nixon's speech writers published the day before Nixon delivered his first inaugural address. "The Men Behind Nixon's Speeches" by William H. Honan appeared in *The New York Times Magazine* on January 19, 1969, and gave a detailed account of the contributions to various Nixon speeches by Raymond Price, William Safire, Patrick Buchanan, and William Gavin. The article discussed private arguments among the writers over language and speech strategy. Specific phrases supplied to Nixon by various members of the speech writing team were cited. Readers of the magazine were encouraged to listen to the coming inaugural for nuances revealing the "rhetorical fingerprints" of the various Nixon writers. Although the tone of the article was sometimes condescending, toward both Nixon and the writers, the story gave the writers public credit for their work. Such credit contrasts sharply with the embarrassment surrounding the discovery of Hamilton's hand in Washington's Farewell Address.

The White House speech writing operation will be discussed more fully in the next chapter, in which the relationship between speaker and writer will be considered. For the purposes of the present topic, it is enough to add that the roster of presidential speech writers has included a number of individuals whose counsel has been valued and whose skills have been appreciated. In addition to the members of the Nixon team, other well known writers in recent years have been McGeorge Bundy, Arthur Schlesinger, Jr., and Theodore Sorensen, who wrote for John F. Kennedy. President Ford reorganized the speech writing staff he inherited from Nixon, and in 1976 he named as his chief writer Robert Orben. Orben had been a top writer of professional humor for such personalities as Red Skelton and Dick Gregory, and he also had experience writing speeches for corporate executives.

Although Adlai Stevenson did not win election to the White House, his race for the office brought out the speech writing talents of poet Archibald MacLeish, historian Bernard DeVota, and playwright Robert Sherwood. Two vice presidents whose speech writers have "gone public" are Spiro Agnew and Nelson Rockefeller.

A final White House note. The most famous, and the most unlikely, speech writer in the twentieth century was Dwight Eisenhower. Although Eisenhower was notorious for the twisted syntax of his presidential news conferences, he had demonstrated considerable speaking skill before his entry into politics and had in fact been a speech writer for General Douglas MacArthur. As a member of MacArthur's staff in the 1930s, Eisenhower contributed to MacArthur's speeches and wrote many of his reports and letters as well.

INTERNATIONAL VIEW OF SPEECH WRITING

The practice of speech writing in Great Britain has always been more circumspect than has been the case in the United States. A first-hand study by Professor J. Jeffrey Auer reported that the average British citizen is not aware of the role of speech writers in English politics and business. Although Prime Minister Margaret Thatcher employed Patrick Cosgrave as her speech writer, the public spotlight did not fall on Mr. Cosgrave the way it frequently has on White House writers.

As demonstrated by seminars on speech writing recently conducted in England and Scotland, a significant amount of speech writing takes place at the corporate level in Britain. The multinational corporation appears to be a likely conduit in continuing to speed North American habits to other countries. Following the American lead in government practices, at least one instance of speech writing can be cited in the Far East where Professor Robert Oliver was for many years a speech writer for officials in the Korean government.

The great bulk of speech writing occurs, of course, not at the highest reaches of government, but at the lower levels of politics or bureaucracy and at the executive level in corporations. A vast number of speech writers work for such figures as ministers of Canadian provinces or governors of states in the U.S. In business, the Chief Executive Officers, the Presidents, and the Vice Presidents of large companies call on their communications departments for speeches.

No "Typical" Speech Writer

There is perhaps no such thing as a "typical" speech writing job. The conditions under which speech writers work and the variety of the tasks they perform make it almost impossible to describe the field. Exceptions exist for almost any general statement, but a few tentative observations may offer some insight into the nature of the speech writing profession.

First, how do people become speech writers? The answer appears to be "by accident." Almost no one who writes speeches for pay will claim to have started out with such a career in mind. Professor Dwight Freshley's survey of speech writers for governors in the United States shows that twenty-nine percent of the writers who responded did their academic work in journalism. [Freshley, p. 97] Professor Otis Baskin conducted a survey in which he found journalism backgrounds for forty-nine percent of the speech writers in corporations he examined and forty-one percent of the public relations firms he questioned. [Baskin, p. 7]

A career change from journalism to speech writing (or, as is often the case, a career expansion to include speech writing as well as journalism) seems to come about because the right skills happen to be in the right place at the right time. Reporters covering political affairs become involved with politicians as press aides and drift into writing speeches. Or the route from journalism to government may be through work in an advertising or public relations agency. In the corporate world someone with a journalism background hired to write and edit company publications may be called on to handle a speech writing assignment.

John Ott, in his book *How To Write And Deliver A Speech*, explains how the process worked in his case. On the day his boss was looking for someone to write a company speech, Ott happened to be the only one in the communications office not working on another project. Although he was a writer for the company's employee magazine and had never written a speech, he got the job. He did it well, and the demand for his new-found talent grew. He was soon the company speech writer. [Ott, pp. 7-8]

Journalism is not the only avenue to speech writing. Some writers have academic backgrounds in English (two percent in the Freshley study), while others studied such fields as speech, history, political science, or economics. Increasingly, writers are being sought among the ranks of those with technical backgrounds in, for instance, computers or engineering.

Few communicators are hired specifically for the task of writing speeches unless they have had experience. As the Ott incident suggests, this experience often comes almost by chance as individuals happen to get speech writing assignments and then, by the cruel rules of a game of survival of the fittest, they either do the job well enough to be called on again or they fail and fall from the ranks.

SELDOM A FULL-TIME TASK

Only a handful of speech writers work at the task as a full-time job. In his study Professor Baskin found that of those employees in corporations who could be identified as speech writers, only twenty percent considered themselves specialists. In the public relations firms he examined, only five percent called speeches their specialty. [Baskin, p. 4]

In one of the most extensive surveys ever made of the speech writing profession, Janine Lichacz discovered barely eleven percent of the speech writers she contacted spent substantially more than seventy-five percent of their time on speech writing duties. Nearly a third of her sample worked at speech writing only about ten percent of their time. Nine writers out of ten in the Lichacz survey worked in the corporate world, as revealed by the additional duties reported. These duties included public relations management, employee communications, press relations, and work on the company annual report. [Lichacz, pp. 84-87]

WRITING FOR MORE THAN ONE SPEAKER

Just as writers seldom work full time on speeches, they do not often write for only one speaker. Quite commonly a writer can be expected to produce speeches for several top officers. Adjusting to the demands of several bosses can be difficult. In one unfortunate situation, a writer handled the speeches for both the president of the company and the CEO. These two officers were rivals for power, and their competition extended to the quality of their speeches. The writer was whipsawed between them as one and then the other demanded more and better speeches.

In a large bureaucracy or a major company, writers may operate in a pool. They are then assigned to write for various speakers on the basis of availability and interests. Such an arrangement often includes a research staff to aid in gathering data. It can be an excellent system to help in avoiding writer burnout.

Some writers occasionally find they are required to produce pattern talks for speaker bureau speakers. Such speeches may be distributed from company headquarters to branches far away. There they are delivered by speakers the writer has never met to audiences unknown to the writer at the time the speeches were prepared. The assumption that these speeches will be adapted to meet local conditions is not something about which a writer can be excessively confident.

SPEECH TOPICS

Speech writers do not write only major addresses dealing with major issues. Writers have the equivalent of what the White House calls "Rose Garden Rubbish." Former presidential speech writer John B. McDonald describes the types of ceremonial speeches the president is called on to give in the Rose Garden:

> Why is the President delighted that Miss Teenage America is calling on him? What does he say to the head of the American Dental Association? What does he tell someone who is off to deliver two musk oxen to the People's Republic of China? What rhetoric is right for the head of an insurance company that has just completed a study of Catholic education? . . . . These are real issues and the President can't wing them—somebody has to develop some background and suggestions for lines of credible commentary. [McDonald, p. A 11]

Writers in business as well as government find many occasions to write similar talks. These would include retirement speeches, factory opening talks, product announcements, and appropriate remarks kicking off a local charity fund drive.

Although the speech writing profession has in it some "old hands" who have had years of experience, the field has many relative beginners. More than half the respondents in the Lichacz study had fewer than five years experience. Only two percent had been writing speeches for twenty years.

Two major explanations can be offered to account for the

fact that speech writers do not appear to stay on the job long. One explanation is that there was a boom in speech writing during the decade of the 1970s. Many of the speech writing jobs surveyed were new positions, and thus the number of years at the task had to be low. It may be that more and more writers will become career speech writers. This possibility will be discussed later.

The second explanation can be found in the difficulty of the speech writing task. Heavy demands are placed on writers and many of them begin to ask to be transferred to a different type of job. Although some writers thrive on the challenges offered by speech writing, others feel much the same as the author of the following indictment of the speech writing career. Because it offers the insights of an experienced writer, this anonymous author's lament is reproduced below in its entirety:

A Speech Writer's Occupational Hazards

"I have been a speech writer for top executives of a large corporation for nearly twenty years now. In my early days I was enthralled by my work, stimulated by the challenges it presented, and still naive enough to feel complimented when I was asked to write a speech for the president of my company.

"But all that has changed. Today, while battling the obligatory mid-life crisis and lamenting my misspent youth, I view my work in a vastly different fashion. Far from being enthralled with it, I am painfully bored by it. Instead of a challenge, it is more often a chore. And I don't feel complimented at all. What I really feel like is a bag man—not all of the time, but certainly a large part of the time and most often just when I am beginning a new speech.

"But I think I am not unusual in my attitude toward my work. Probably most speech writers feel this way from time to time. Those who feel most negatively about their work are those who have been exposed for the longest period of time to five occupational hazards of the job. There may be more than five, but of these I speak with experience and passion.

Anonymity

"From the beginning, the unwritten rule in speech writing

has been that the writer must remain anonymous. Most of us honor that tradition. Although we may admit to some of our closest friends that we authored this or that speech, to most others who ask we manage a Mona Lisa smile and say that we merely did some research for the speaker. When the speech hasn't gone over well, of course, we don't mind disclaiming it and we do so with perhaps more force than necessary. But when a speech has brought the audience to its feet in rousing ovation, that's when it is hardest not to claim some credit for it. Then the writer wants to say, 'You're mighty right I wrote that speech. Didn't that analogy knock you out! Wasn't that illustration right on target! How about those smooth transitions! And what a conclusion!' That's what we would like to say, but instead we restrain ourselves and simply join in the applause, reflecting momentarily perhaps on the unfairness of it all.

"But I need to distinguish here between anonymity and appreciation. No speech writer expects the audience to cry 'Author, Author' at the conclusion of a speech. Nor does he expect, as Edwin Newman has suggested, that the speaker either open or conclude with the statement, 'This speech was based on an idea by. . . .'

"Most of us do not want or need public acclaim. What we do want is appreciation for the work we do, especially from the speaker for whom we do it. That appreciation often is not forthcoming. We also want to be able to acknowledge, at least within our company or firm, the kind of work we do. We are not Watergate Plumbers, after all; our work is not something to be ashamed of. And it is demoralizing to spend one's entire career being nonspecific and hedging about one's job. It is also depersonalizing, dehumanizing, and all those other things which whittle away at self-confidence and make it all that much harder to write good speeches. Anonymity is definitely an occupational hazard of the speech writer.

ISOLATION

"The old saying that 'Writing is a lonely job' is true. But I think speech writing is the loneliest of all. Other kinds of writers can enjoy the camaraderie of their colleagues, but we speech writers usually don't even know who our colleagues are.

"Now I realize that we are not so specialized that we cannot speak to and be understood by other writers or PR personnel. But somehow it's just not quite the same as sharing the problems and frustrations of the job with another of your own kind.

"But professional isolation is not the only problem; physical isolation is a problem for the speech writer as well. This may be a problem peculiar only to my own personality, but it is one I have to guard against most carefully. When I am writing a speech, I am totally immersed in it. 'Enmeshed' may be a better word, At any rate, I am preoccupied to the extent that I become antisocial. The longer I wrestle with the problem of how to construct the speech, the more I cut myself off from contact with other people and the more depressed I become. The deeper the depression, the harder it is to work, and so the cycle goes. This is a problem for the speech writer I think because as any psychiatrist will tell you, if you want to demoralize and depress someone, one way to do that is to isolate them. Hence the fear of ostracism in our society or of solitary confinement in prisons. Isolation can be an energy-sapping hazard to the speech writer. The remedy, I've found, is to break the cycle at any point and just go talk with someone.

STAYING TOO LONG IN THE JOB

"The problem here is obvious. For the first several months or even years in the speech writing job, you bring a fresh approach to your topics. You haven't yet used up all your jokes or illustrations. You haven't learned what you can't do because of certain policies or regulations. And you haven't had to write on the same topics so often that you can no longer think of anything new to say about them. But after a time, you exhaust your reserves and become a burnt-out case. For me that happened after about five years on the same job writing for the same speaker.

"The trick in speech writing is not to write one speech or two speeches. Just about anyone can do that. The real trick is to write the third, fourth, fifth, and sixth speech all on the same topic and to make them all interesting. That's tough, because you quickly reach the point where you spend more time desperately wondering what else you can possibly say on the subject than you do in actually saying it. And for me at least, it's almost impossible to write a good speech in a mood of desperation.

"Sometimes, however, it isn't necessary to actually leave the job or to change jobs. A short stint at a different kind of writing, or writing for a different speaker may help restore your fine cutting edge. But I'm afraid nothing will help your creativity for writing United Way or Savings Bonds speeches year after year. If that's your lot, just tell yourself that's what you get paid for and go ahead and do it. You may also console yourself with the thought that nobody will know whether your speech this year is too much like last year's. They don't remember last year's speech and they won't remember this year's either.

THE DEMAND NATURE OF THE JOB

"As a speech writer for executives, you're in business to provide a service at the demand of your client. Consequently, try though you might, it's difficult to spread your workload evenly. For example, last month I had only two speeches due this month. It looked like a pretty easy schedule and I even thought about taking a few days off. But in just two day's time, my client accepted four additional speaking engagements, all in one week. So instead of an easy month with vacation time, I've worked right down to the wire, at night and through the weekends. That's to be expected occasionally, but after a time you become exhausted and that's when it becomes a hazard. Any writer needs some down time—time to read, time to clean out files, time to let the mind lie fallow. If you don't have that time, the quality of your work will suffer and so will you. You'll also come to hate your job.

HAVING TO WRITE ON SUBJECTS YOU COULDN'T CARE LESS ABOUT

"I've saved this hazard for last because I think it's the most lethal of all. To me there are few things more exhausting than having to reach down within myself and generate enthusiasm for something that inherently bores me stiff. But that is often the lot of the speech writer. Your topics are dictated not by you but by your speaker. You rarely get to write on what you know most about or enjoy most, and it's hard to write an interesting talk on a subject you don't find interesting. Imagine having to write talk after talk on the Salt II agreements, for example, or on the Social Responsibility of Business, or on Why You Should Buy U. S. Savings Bonds. If you're interested in those topics, fine. But if you're as saturated with them as I am, the only thing worse would be to have to write the 'Don't Squeeze the Charmin' commercials. Nothing could be worse than that.

"Assignments like those have done more to wear me down to a nub than any of the other hazards I've mentioned altogether. But face it: this is not something we can do much about. Such is the essence of our craft, our reason for being on the payroll. Given enough time for research and thought, we are supposed to be able to write interestingly on any subject and to present the best case for our client that we possibly can. That is the responsibility of the advocate and that is our job.

"If there is anything we can do to help ourselves and guard against the hazards of being a professional speech writer, it is to recognize our limitations and refuse to take ourselves too seriously. No one can write one outstanding speech after another, especially when you're isolated and anonymous, when you're burned out and bored, or when you have to create an artificial enthusiasm for your topic. All those things just make you a bona fide speech writer. Besides, if you turn out a lousy speech now and then, who knows, you may get out of this crummy job."

The above reflections focus only on the most pessimistic aspects of speech writing. But most writers encounter some of the problems cited at least occasionally. However, hardly any writer (not even the person who wrote the criticism) feels completely negative all the time.

CAREER PLANNING FOR THE SPEECH WRITER

Indeed, many communicators consider speech writing an excellent career and others regard it as a likely ladder to a management position.

In attempting to answer the question, "Is there life after manuscript?," Wesley Poriotis has identified some of the factors favoring advancement in management for the speech writer.

Drawing on his experience as a management consultant who finds positions for speech writers in top corporations, Poriotis noted the following advantages possessed by the speech writer: (1) Involvement in policy formation, (2) Experience in clear and analytical thinking, (3) Negotiating skills learned in working with speakers and others, and (4) Extensive knowledge of the company acquired in writing speeches. [Poriotis, pp. 22-23]

There are some disadvantages. Some writers think of their work in narrow, technical terms. They regard themselves as wordsmiths and fail to become involved in communication strategy. Such writers are especially likely to become isolated from the rest of their organization, and they do not take advantage of the opportunities offered by their position to build useful contacts.

One ironic disadvantage for the speech writer seeking advancement grows out of the shortage of qualified writers. A speaker may be reluctant to see a writer move into management because of the difficulty of finding a replacement. As one speech writer remarked wryly, "My boss says I can't quit; I'm too good."

THE MARKET

While speech writing can be a means for advancing to a management post, it can also be seen as a rewarding career in itself. The salary policies of many corporations have in the past been a serious obstacle to speech writing careers. When promotion and salary are based in a significant degree on the number of subordinates a person has, speech writers do not always appear to be important "managers." Emphasis on the managerial criterion for reward at the expense of attention to what we might call a talent criterion may be changing in the corporate world.

A comparison has often been made between the talent supplied by communications experts in business and the talent supplied by actors, singers, and sports figures to employers or clients. Increasingly, corporations appear willing to recognize that salary cannot always be based on how many people fit below someone's name on an organizational chart.

Leading the way in establishing higher salary levels are the writers for top corporate executives. Writers with as little as five to ten years experience who are able to land jobs as full-time writers for presidents and vice presidents of major companies command salaries, in 1982 dollars, in the $50s, $60s, and $70s.

Even jobs which require only part-time speech writing or jobs in which the writing is done in smaller companies or for executives below the top rank, salaries for speech writers are likely to be higher than those for other communications jobs. Lichacz estimated, on the basis of the data from her survey, that speech writers were paid $3,000 per year more than the average in the public relations field. James Busse, gathering his information primarily from interviews, concluded that speech writers ranked with those at the top of the salary scale in public relations. [Busse, p. 60] The increasing demand for speeches can be expected to keep pressure on the market to hold speech writing salaries at a high level.

CHANGING JOBS

One reflection of the prevailing market situation is the number of management consultants, such as Wesley Poriotis, who specialize in placing speech writers. Jean Cardwell in Chicago along with Bill Cantor and Larry Marshall in New York all report more openings for speech writers than writers to fill the openings. The names and addresses of these recruiters appear following the bibliography at the end of this book.

Speech writers will find it advisable to keep up to date on the employment picture. A corporate merger, the transfer of a boss to a new company, or any number of unforeseen circumstances may dictate a job change. Because speech writers have no specialized professional association and no regular meetings and conferences to attend with their peers, special effort may be required to stay informed.

A surprising number of speech writers do not bother to keep copies of the speeches they write. At least a few samples should be retained, and occasionally successive drafts would prove interesting in a private personnel file. A complete list of speeches produced should be kept. Congratulatory letters and memos should not be discarded, and a few news clippings might prove valuable in a job interview. If records are not maintained, the hazard of anonymity that plagues a writer's work can also be a barrier to establishing credentials for a new position.

THE SPEECH WRITING PERSONALITY

A few years ago an effort was made to describe "the authoritarian personality." The effort was later largely discredited. The same fate would befall anyone who decided to describe the personality traits possessed by speech writers. They fit no pattern. Some are talkative, but others, as one company communications director tactfully put it, are "not highly verbal" in a nonprofessional situation. As a group they are tidy and unkempt, serious and flippant, casual and formal, and eager and cautious. A few of them keep their desk tops clean. Many of them will quickly and somewhat sarcastically reject the suggestion that they "must love words." Most of them find they think more clearly and work more efficiently with a deadline staring them in the face. But there's no such thing as a speech writer personality.

The abilities needed by a speech writer are another matter. An ear for the sound of language distinguishes all truly good speech writers. So does a capacity for synthesis, the crucial capacity to draw material from disparate sources to produce a coherent talk. Willingness to work long and uncertain hours is a must. Skill at getting along with people who are in too big a hurry to give out needed information helps. Knowing how to see things from the speaker's perspective (how to become a clone, according to an oil company speech writer) comes easily to most good speech writers.

If all else fails in an attempt to identify a speech writer, watch one in the act of writing. They often move their lips.

CHAPTER II

RELATIONSHIP BETWEEN SPEAKER AND WRITER

"A good speech cannot be interchangeable. Rather it must accurately reflect the speaker's individuality by giving his personal reaction to a problem or an issue. . . . This means that the chief executive must collaborate with his public affairs department or his speechwriter. All too often the chief executive expects a speech to appear magically on his desk without any contribution on his part." [*Wall Street Journal,* June 13, 1975, quoted from a report by Burson-Marsteller]

A good working environment can increase efficiency in almost any job, but nowhere do working conditions affect the quality of the product more than in speech writing. The actual writing of a speech may be a lonely act, but the cooperation and understanding of many people will usually be required if the speech is to be a success. Writers need to acknowledge the special conditions that surround their work, and they must determine how hard they are willing to press in order to build or maintain creative, productive working relationships.

Three matters demand attention: direct speaker contact, adequate writing time, and access to information.

CONTACT WITH SPEAKER

Countless speeches have been ruined because the speakers did not find time to work closely with their speech writers. And a great deal of extra labor has gone into the revision process because a writer's first communication from a speaker, coming after the completion of a first draft, was "This is not what I want at all!"

Speaking is too personal a matter to permit a writer to work in isolation from the person who is to give the talk. Every writer wishes to have the ability, as Ted Sorensen had with John F.

28

Kennedy, to be an alter ego for a speaker, to know how the speaker feels and thinks. But Sorensen had access to Kennedy, and it is that direct access that allows a writer to develop the required insights into a speaker's psyche. A conference between speaker and writer should be held as soon as possible after a speaking engagement is accepted. The speaker should make clear to the writer precisely the subject matter the speaker wants to cover, and the goal of the speech should be clarified.

BEWARE THE FLUNKY

Writers must vigorously resist any efforts of an intermediary to represent the speaker's views. Rarely will this addition of a link in the communications chain prove workable. Only personal contact will reveal to the writer an accurate picture of the speaker's intentions. Sitting across the desk or in the next seat on an airplane, the writer picks up many nonverbal clues. The speaker's tone of voice and facial expression will often tell more than mere words can convey.

Unfortunately, the motives of the intermediary are not always the highest. Major executives often allow themselves to become surrounded with layers of flunkies who see their task as that of protecting the boss from people the flunky regards as unimportant. In this process, the flunky may expect to gain by keeping the status of the speech writer low. One speech writer characterizes this problem as springing from the "territorial imperatives of other managers who perhaps all too well understand the relationship that often develops between a speaker and a speech writer."

Quite often an administrative flunky will speak forcefully in claiming to represent the speaker's views accurately. This decisive demeanor quickly fades, however, when a draft of a speech is rejected. The fault will fall on the shoulders of the writer and not on the once confident individual who claimed to know exactly what the boss wanted.

FOLLOW-UP CONFERENCES

After an initial conference to set the direction of the speech, the writer begins to complete an audience analysis, gather data, and write a first draft. An understanding that the writer's phone calls will be put through to the speaker can be most helpful in this period if the writer needs to touch base at some point. A second formal conference should be held after the speaker has a chance to read the first draft.

Any changes the speaker wants should be discussed directly with the writer. Additional conferences should follow if any other drafts prove necessary. As soon as it appears that a substantial amount of the speech is acceptable, the speaker should read the speech aloud with the writer present to allow for fine tuning of language.

Writers need a high degree of skill in interpersonal communication to hold a satisfactory conference. Because the speaker is an important person whose time is valuable, the writer may be too quick to accept a statement from the speaker without fully understanding it. Especially in the initial meeting, the writer must get a correct reading of the speaker's intent. This may call for a number of statements of the let's-see-if-I-have-this-straight sort. Also, the writer must know when to accept a vague response as an indication that the writer has leeway to decide a particular issue because the speaker either does not know or does not care what should be said. At the end of a conference the writer should have a good set of notes.

In the follow-up conferences, a writer should not too quickly accept abrupt and arbitrary changes. If the initial conference laid a solid foundation for the speech, the writer should attempt to return to that foundation. Reference to notes and citations of the speaker's original instructions may prevent a great deal of hard work from being wasted. Of course, the writer should be alert for genuine improvements, even if they are major. And if the speaker is adamant about capricious changes, the writer naturally can do little other than comply.

A final pre-speech conference for at least some major speeches should include a dress rehearsal of the speech. Some suggestions will be offered in a later chapter on working with the speaker on delivery.

As often as possible, a speech writer should hear the speech delivered and hold a post-speech conference with the speaker. Far too many speech writers get only vague secondhand reports on how the speech fared with an audience. Hearing the speech as it is presented gives a writer much valuable information. The actual response of the audience can be compared with the response the writer expected to get, although the contrast may shock the writer. Humor that sounded fine in the office may fail badly (or a light quip may get a much better than expected reaction). A passage in the talk may get enough overt positive reaction to suggest it could be worked into other speeches.

A tape recorder may give some of the clues the writer needs and is better than nothing at all. But as General Motors speech writer W. M. Lovell points out, "The only half-way reliable method for discovering individual quirks is to listen while the person makes the speech. The only completely reliable way is to hear that person make several speeches." [Lovell, p. 12]

A talk with the speaker on the day following the speech, or for that matter on the way home after the presentation, gives the writer a chance to offer suggestions on delivery and to get a reading of the speaker's degree of satisfaction with the talk. Especially in the case of a relaxed conversation on the plane, many opportunities may arise to build a stronger speaker-writer relationship.

WORKING WITH THE SPEAKER: A CASE HISTORY

Are the above suggestions realistic? Are they practiced by successful writers and speakers? Unfortunately, the answer is "only sometimes." But when a speaker thinks a speaking opportunity is of great importance, considerable interaction may occur between the speaker and the writer. The following case history illustrates such an instance. The speaker, Florida governor Reubin Askew, had been tapped to give the Keynote Address at the 1972 Democratic National Convention. Professors Sara Newell and Tom King traced the history of the writing of the speech; their findings are summarized below. [Newell, pp. 346-358]

The speech was written by the governor's speech writer, Roland Page, with the aid of the governor's press secretary and the governor's senior executive assistant. After he got the assignment, Page accompanied Governor Askew on a business trip so they could discuss what the governor wished to say. Even with extensive contact with the governor, Page was aware when he submitted the first draft that he had not captured the essense of what his speaker wanted. He was therefore not surprised when, in a conference with the writing staff, the governor cut out four-fifths of the first effort.

Page then produced a second draft which was discussed at an involved and most unusual speaker-writer conference. Askew arranged a two-day meeting at a hideaway beach cottage where he and the three writers turned out the third draft of the speech. So intense was their work that when the power failed one night they continued to work with the aid of a kerosene lantern.

The beach cottage draft became the foundation for the final version of the speech, although a total of nine drafts were finally produced. The fourth draft, for example, introduced the "zingers" that were to key the applause at the convention. The fifth and sixth drafts involved only routine changes in language and structure. As each of these drafts was finished, the governor and his speech writing staff held a conference. They discussed changes and Askew read each successive draft aloud.

The last three versions of speech resulted from changes made on the plane and at the convention in Miami Beach. And with all this careful preparation behind him, the governor made sixty-seven minor alterations as he delivered the speech.

ADEQUATE WRITING TIME

A speech writer once remarked ruefully, "My boss confuses writing time with typing speed." Anyone who has never written a speech may have difficulty appreciating the complexity of the task and the amount of time required to get it done. Some speeches are easier to write than others, of course, and no precise answer can be given to answer the question, "How long does it take to write a speech?"

It is not unusual, however, for a good writer to spend an hour for every minute of delivery time. And that does not count research time. The "hour per minute" guide deals only with organizing, writing, thinking, and rewriting; it assumes that the facts needed for the speech are on hand or that the time required to gather them will not be counted in the customary writing time.

Two Dimensions of Time

In planning a writing schedule for an assignment, writers should recognize two distinct dimensions of time. In addition to the actual writing time, consideration should be given to the period of time over which a speech is written. It is one thing to write a speech in a fourteen hour blitz (say from ten o'clock on Sunday morning until midnight) and quite another to distribute the work throughout a normal week in blocks of time ranging from one to four hours in length.

A given speech may be written in one uninterrupted period; that sometimes is the best way. But not always. Frequently writers benefit from the opportunity to turn to another task and return to the speech refreshed. A walk in the park or an hour of relaxed browsing in the public library may be legitimate alternative activities that will aid in producing a better speech.

Speech writing is a creative activity, and we do not yet fully understand how the human brain functions with such activities. Some research suggests a fuller appreciation of the separate capacities of the brain's hemispheres will help writers work more efficiently. Some writers believe if your writing is going very badly, the wrong hemisphere is in control, and you should shift for a time to some more mundane task.

Writers' Block

When the dread writers' block strikes, you may not be able to afford to break away. Over the years writers have developed many stratagems to combat this problem. Some find that dictating works better than writing. Others insist that a time and place be set aside for writing, and that you force yourself to write no matter how trite or even nonsensical your material proves to be.

One useful suggestion is to treat the speech writing task as incremental. Divide a given speech writing job into parts, perhaps even going so far as to maintain separate file folders for each part. Then if you get stuck, say, in writing the opening, you go on to work on the first point or the conclusion. If your writing is going well but you lack a needed statistic or quotation, leave a blank space and keep on going. The trick is to avoid letting a barrier for any one part of the speech become a barrier for the speech as a whole.

No incentive to completing a speech compares with the motivation supplied by a deadline. The adrenaline flows, the words come, and somehow the speech that couldn't be written yesterday can be written today. The magical power of the deadline cannot be denied, but no one should conclude that it is unnecessary to plan for adequate writing time spread over a reasonable period of days or weeks. If sufficient time has been set aside to write the speech, the writer has the luxury of using the incentive supplied by a deadline to make a few incisive revisions in the manuscript. Even when the well planned speech is completed in a flurry of activity minutes before the boss is scheduled to get it, that speech will quite likely have benefited from the incubation time and reflection time allowed by having a good writing schedule.

ADEQUATE WRITING TIME: A CASE HISTORY

A power company in the northwestern United States has developed a sound procedure for allowing enough time to write speeches. The system they use is set forth in the memo below. The names of individuals have been omitted, but the text of the memo has not been changed:

TO: Manager, Communications
FROM: Speech Writer
SUBJECT: Preparation of Speeches

"In order to have a speech in final form 10 days in advance of its presentation, it is necessary that:

1. I be notified of the date the speech is to be given about six weeks in advance.
2. Sufficient work time be allocated exclusively for preparation of the speech.

"An ideal typical schedule would be as follows:

1. Notification of date of speech
2. Researching the location, audience, local facts   (2-3 days)
3. Contact program chair to determine topic   (1-2 days)
4. Confer with the speaker to determine how topic should be approached and to determine whether slides or other visuals should be used

5.	Research topic—select slides	(5 days)
6.	Prepare speech	(5 days)
7.	Review by speaker and others affected	(5 days)
8.	Corrections or rewrite	(1 day)
9.	Final review by speaker	(2-3 days)
10.	Final preparation and typing	(1 day)

"While the total time involved is 22 to 25 working days, the speech would be on the speaker's desk for preliminary review 10 days before it is to be given.

"This schedule does not mean that speeches must be scheduled six weeks apart. It means primarily that I must know that far ahead of time so that the work can proceed in an orderly fashion. More than one could be done at the same time and with the development of a good, basic speech, the research and preparation time could be shortened.

"Each speech is tailored to a specific audience. In speaking to groups such as Chambers of Commerce, Kiwanis, Rotary or other service clubs, the speaker's credibility is enhanced if he knows some facts about the geographic area, or the town, and can make some local references. This involves contacting persons in the club, or the local utility to obtain the information.

"It is also necessary to obtain information on the meeting itself, i.e., the date, time, length of time allowed for the speech, the size and composition of the audience, the meeting place and the master of ceremonies.

"The amount of time required for research depends upon the topic. If it is a simple 'Company Story' type of speech, research time is minimal.

"If it is a more technical speech, assistance may be needed from the technical staff and extra time must be allowed.

"To determine a topic, it is necessary, in many cases, to confer with the program chair to determine the wishes of the audience.

"It is vital that I confer with the speaker to discuss the topic and the manner in which it is to be approached, as well as whether there will be visual aids.

"Writing of the speech takes a minimum of one week. Another week should be allowed for review by others to assure accuracy of figures or statements. This has not always been done, but it is recommended.

"Time must be allowed for rewriting or corrections, final review and final typing.

"It would also be a service if the speech could be reproduced to use as a handout for the media reporters. And, if there is sufficient time, a news release could be prepared for distribution on the day of the speech.

"The critical factors involved in having a speech prepared 10 days in advance are that there is sufficient advance notice and that sufficient time can be allocated exclusively for work on the speech.

"Without this, the schedule fails."

Access to Information

Just as editors of corporate and government publications must contend with something called the approval process, so must the speech writer submit drafts of speeches to a variety of people and departments to check for accuracy of data and possible violations of standing policy. The writer's first problem in circulating drafts of speeches is to keep in control of the process.

The Route the Speech Travels

The speech writer should fight to enforce one cardinal rule: no one must be allowed to tamper with the manuscript as it travels from writer to speaker and back again. All suggestions for change, and for that matter any orders to change, should go directly to the speech writer for incorporation in the manuscript.

Figure 1 illustrates a clear pathway between the writer and the speaker. While the manuscript may travel to the desk of an engineer, a CPA, and/or a lawyer, it always returns to the writer before it goes on to the speaker. Even the writer's editor or supervisor, who may well insist on seeing the final copy before it goes forward, should make no unilateral changes.

The reasons for this procedure are obvious. There must be a consistency of style in a speech that can hardly be present if several experts decide to rewrite passages of the talk. And only the writer in a well-organized operation has spoken directly to the speaker about the proposed content and aim of the speech. Also, the writer cannot maintain a solid working relationship with a speaker if the text reaching the speaker has more to do with power struggles in the organization than with the writer's skill.

Word Molesters

Even the best organized system will not protect a writer from the urge of advisors to meddle gratuitously with the language of the draft of a speech. Handling these word molesters calls for confidence and courage on the part of a writer. Technical experts are likely offenders. They sometimes value the preciseness of their jargon over the goal of being understood by an audience.

Fig. 1

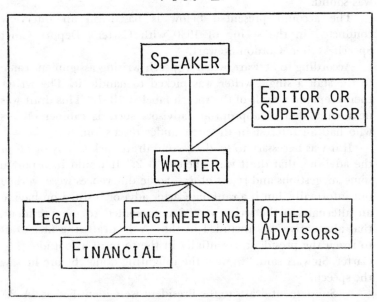

The Manuscript Route

Financial experts often have a language of their own, and lawyers occasionally write in a language only remotely similar to English.

When the changes occur, as they often do, in parts of the speech unrelated to the advisor's area of competence, the writer can easily ignore the suggestions. When the proposed changes involve scientific or legal matters, some effort at compromise may be in order. At the very least, a properly structured communications office will not allow advisors to change words without the writer's knowledge. The writer then has a chance to make an argument for replacing the jargon with lucid prose.

White House Example

President Jimmy Carter, with a methodical approach to the problem, had a well-organized White House speech writing staff. Although at one point Carter's chief speech writer resigned with some pointed criticisms of the president [Fallows, pp. 33-35].

the process used by the writers in gathering and using information was sound.

The account presented below is based on an interview conducted in the spring of 1980 with Carter's Deputy Chief Speech Writer, Gordon Stewart.

According to Stewart, when a speech writing assignment came to the staff a single writer was picked to handle it. The writer then prepared a draft of the speech labeled "B–1." This draft was next circulated to appropriate advisors such as cabinet officers who had an interest in the area under discussion.

If it was necessary to send a second draft back to any or all of the advisors, that draft was labeled "B–2." It would incorporate some suggestions and reject others. Some differences were worked out informally, but if a ranking Carter advisor insisted on having an alternate to the writer's version presented to the president, that alternative was included in the "A–1" draft, the first draft to reach the president, essentially in the form of a footnote. Mr. Carter, Stewart said, "wanted the infighting done" before he saw the speech.

Subsequent drafts to the President were identified as "A–2," "A–3," and so on until a final draft won approval. Stewart noted that under President Carter a few drafts were usually sufficient.

Positive Features of the Approval Process

The approval process has its problems, but the writer can often benefit from suggestions and corrections. Writers often find it advisable to cultivate a network of experts and advisors who can later offer valuable help on a speech.

Usually it is wise to build a relationship with potential contributors to speeches before they are actually needed. Rather than telephoning someone at the last minute or abruptly depositing a manuscript on the desk of someone you have never met, you might choose to get acquainted with people who will be useful to you.

Anyone who helps in the writing of a speech should get some feedback from the writer. If you call on someone in research and development for data, let that person know how useful the information was in writing the speech. A memo with a copy of the final draft may help make it easier to get assistance the next time you need it.

Writers frequently encounter a reluctance on the part of some to divulge information. After all, knowledge is power, and few people want to surrender what they may regard as highly confidential facts about plans for a new product or the expected impact of a management decision. The writer is faced with the delicate problem of bringing the power of the speaker's official position to bear on a reluctant guardian of facts without destroying the possibility of friendly and willing cooperation. Again, attention to building good channels of communication in advance will prove useful. But it may be that the writer will need to learn to take an assertive stance.

THE ASSERTIVE WRITER

Writers must determine how forward they wish to be in attempting to affect their working conditions. Because so few people understand the speech writing process, little is likely to be done to improve it if the writer does not speak out. The question then becomes, how assertive will the writer be?

Some writers have made their peace with their jobs and have given up trying to establish a productive work environment. They work with little or no speaker contact, write speeches hastily when adequate notice could have been given, and settle for a minimum of solid material to include in their speeches.

Other writers insist on a good working relationship as a condition for staying on the job. If they cannot improve conditions, they quit. Some leave quietly, and some, like Robert Shrum in departing the campaign of Jimmy Carter, go out with a blast. [Shrum, pp. 34-40]

Most writers, of course, fall somewhere in the middle. They don't passively accept their fate, but they don't make demands that will lead to separation. Such writers simply look for all opportunities to push for changes. In some cases speakers simply have not been asked, or have not been asked often enough, for more conferences with their writers. It may be the writer's supervisor who is reluctant to make the request or who does not understand its importance. In the case of getting inadequate notice of a speaking engagement, it may be that no one has bothered to try to improve communication between the speaker and the writer. Or perhaps it has never occurred to anyone that the speech writer should attend meetings where important issues are being decided, meetings which would give the writer useful facts as well as provide an opportunity to observe the speaker talking off the cuff.

In short, writers should look for opportunities to improve their situations. Staff meetings or performance reviews may provide an opening for a frank discussion of needed changes. Writers can set forth their needs in memos or position papers.

In some cases a consultant may be brought in to examine the speech writing process. The outside consultant's opinion may have more weight than internal opinion, and many consultants are qualified to address the problem. The firm of Burson-Marsteller, for example, has developed a booklet describing its conviction that speech writing should not be considered in isolation but should be viewed as part of "a systems approach." [Burson-Marsteller, pp. 25-33]

THE SPEECH WRITER AS POLICY MAKER

A successful relationship with a speaker depends in part on the writer's full understanding that speech writing is more than dressing up someone else's ideas. As Chrysler speech writer Charles Connolley observed, "In my case, when my client is Mr. Iacocca, I have to become a surrogate chairman. When I have to write the top man's speech, I'm literally forced to figure out policy, compress it, and make it cogent from the point of view of the Chairman. Therefore, when I sit in on meetings to dig for my information, I'm not just a recorder, I'm a strategist." Or, as a top writer at another major company put it, "Often top management does not create policy at all in a formal sense. . . . management may have only vague ideas on a subject. These ideas will often be clarified, stated and established in a policy form only through a business speech." [Poriotis, p. 22]

Speech writers, then, do not act as mere parrots. They often find themselves deeply involved in decisionmaking. Any writer who works for an official who speaks in public for an organization may help form policy. This comes about in three ways.

PHRASING POLICY

First, a writer may merely phrase a policy. The speech writer functions in this role as articulator. A company or agency policy may never have been committed to paper. When the writing process begins, the subtle nuances of language become apparent. The writer must put into print that which has been drifting about in oral form. Drafts of such a speech may produce long arguments over a word or a clause. Eventually the writer must sit down and hammer out a speech that puts the organization on record.

Many corporations recognize that speeches become a printed record of company policy. General Electric publishes executive speeches in a format that permits ready filing and easy retrieval. The speeches are distributed with catalogue code numbers on the back page, and they have punched holes in the margin to permit them to be kept in order.

FORCING A POLICY

At some point in the process of speech preparation, a writer may shift from the role of articulator of policy and become the catalyst who forces a policy into being. The writer may simply be unable to complete a passage on government regulation or environmental safeguards without having someone determine the company's official position. Just as the President of the United States did not have a position on the social significance of Miss Teenage America, the President of Ajax Widgets may not have a position on the company's support for tax reform until called on to deliver a speech on the subject.

FORMULATING A POLICY

Documented cases of speech writers actively playing the role of policy maker are easier to find in politics than in business writing. This may be because political writers are more aggressive in their demands than corporate writers, or it may be that political writers are simply less modest in their claims.

Whatever the explanation, political writers are often quite open about discussing their influence on their speakers. Speech writer Mel Grayson, for instance, boasted that a major shift in federal government policy on price controls was "mine, all mine, and mine alone." [Grayson, p. 65] Grayson said that he put the policy statement in a Houston speech by Vice President Agnew without any guidance from White House policy advisors, and Grayson speculated that his idea became the basis for other official statements and perhaps for actual changes in market prices.

Robert Shrum, who was one of the speech writers for the widely noted 1981 Democratic Convention speech by Teddy Kennedy, has written for a number of major politicians including Edmund Muskie. In his efforts to get Muskie to come out in opposition to military aid for Vietnam, Shrum repeatedly wrote into the senator's speeches statements taking that position. Finally worn down by his speech writer, Muskie gave up. As Shrum described it, "It took eight months of putting it in speeches and getting it knocked out, of arguing with him, of slowly turning Clifford and Warnke around by getting them to think it was their idea." [Devlin, p. 10]

CHANGING PERCEPTIONS

While corporate writers are generally more guarded in relating the details of their influence, Mel Grayson is no doubt right in correcting the public impression of speech writers as "intellectual stenographers." One indication that corporations are recognizing the policy role of speech writers can be found in subtle changes in the language corporations use in referring to speech writers.

More and more frequently, the word "policy" appears in job titles and in department names. W. M. Lovell, for example, is GM's Director of Policy Coordination, and Frank Stokes of Monsanto is Director of Policy Analysis and Communication. Writers of speeches have suffered for years under titles apparently designed in some cases to obscure rather than clarify the speech writing task. "Editorial Assistant" and "Communication Specialist" are not titles likely to indicate power or to confer status.

Advertisements for jobs also contain language reflecting an awareness of the speech writer as more than a parrot of someone else's ideas. Here are some samples from recent issues of *The Effective Speech Writer's Newsletter*: writer "will be involved with planning and developing themes and messages;" "accessibility to top management and opportunity to take on the tough issues go along with the job;" and "help needed in articulating company's social concern."

SPECIAL CONSIDERATIONS

WRITING BY COMMITTEE

There is merit in Ted Sorensen's contention that "group authorship is rarely if ever successful," because, as he goes on to point out, "A certain continuity and precision of style, and unity of argument must be carefully drafted. . . ." [Sorensen, p. 61] The fact remains, however, that many speeches will involve the hand of more than one writer.

There are actually some advantages to having more than one writer working on a talk. As Joseph Persico, once a speech writer for Nelson Rockefeller, noted, there are occasions when "speech-writers might visit each other's cubicles and try to strike creative sparks off one another." [Persico, p. 59] And Persico commented favorably on the advantages of having a chief speech writer who served as editor and could, based on long experience with the speaker, make changes in a writer's copy to make sure the language fit the Rockefeller style. An editor, as in the case of any type of writing, may well be the speech writer's best friend. Phillips Petroleum Company is among the corporations that have smoothly functioning writing staffs with excellent relations between editors and speech writers.

Editing is a term that might be applied to much of the work speech writers do. Often a writer starts a speech with a great deal of material written by someone else or by a number of other writers. This material could include financial statements, reports, articles, or even previously delivered speeches. The writer's task may be less to create than to combine. In the process the uniformity of style Sorensen mentioned must be imposed.

In addition to the unseen and perhaps unknown persons who supply the speech writer with raw material for a speech, there will at times be more than one writer at work on a given speech. When this happens, early coordination among writers can be most helpful. Dr. Lois Einhorn has experimented with various approaches to group writing. She found groups were more successful when they began with a "prewriting conference" than when they worked separately and attempted to merge their individual work into a single draft. Joseph Persico found in working with Rockefeller that a "story conference," held soon after a speaking calendar was established, was useful both in generating ideas for speeches and in coordinating efforts of the writers.

FREE-LANCE WRITING

Working as a free-lance speech writer creates a special relationship between writer and speaker. In spite of some of its problems, the free-lance approach has great appeal to both writers and speakers.

From the writer's point of view, writing speeches "off duty" may provide needed variety and challenge. As an opportunity to make additional money, it has the advantage of being done privately and it can fit into odd moments of available time.

The advantages from an organization's perspective are often even more compelling. Since a speaking schedule is sometimes unbalanced with periods of intense activity, a free-lance writer may be a welcome solution to the problem of overload. Some organizations may find the free-lance approach a permanent solution to their speech writing needs, even if a large number of speeches is needed. The problems of company infighting, which have been alluded to, are avoided to a large degree. When the writer is an outsider on temporary assignment, sensitivity about the pecking order will be lessened.

The financial arrangements can be advantageous to both parties. A company will not have a permanent employee drawing a full salary plus benefits. And the writer can expect to be paid at least at the same rate as the full-time job the writer holds.

Admittedly, fees for free-lance speech writing vary considerably. One writer offers pre-packaged commencement speeches for about $25. In another case a public relations firm charged $50,000 for a single speech. In that instance the firm claimed to have lost money because the speech was given in a foreign country with simultaneous translation and was accompanied by a sophisticated multi-media presentation. Obviously, most fees fall somewhere between these extremes. When research time is added to writing time, $1500 to $2000 is not unusual for a fairly typical fifteen to twenty minute speech.

FACILITIES

It is easy to describe the ideal speech writer's office. It is private with a relaxing view. It is equipped with a word processor. Files bulge with choice bits of data the writer has socked away. A research staff is located nearby with a computer that quickly calls up the latest statistics. There is a sofa suitable for a couple of hours sleep when the writer has to work all night.

CONCLUSION

Perhaps no speech writer has ideal working conditions. But to return to the White House example, the evidence of the past four decades suggests the very best speakers fully recognize the importance of speech writing and involve themselves in the speech writing process. As Rosenman reports, FDR's schedule fell one or two days behind when he worked with his writers on a major speech. [Rosenman, p. 12] Bob Orben recalls from his days as Jerry Ford's head speech writer that

> President Ford gave an estimated 1200 speeches during his term of office and all were conceived, developed, rewritten, and polished based on his direction and guidance received from meetings in the Oval Office. We usually had two meetings a week with President Ford. One to discuss the concept and content of future speeches. A second to review, page by page, drafts of immediately upcoming speeches. We knew precisely what he liked, what he didn't like, and what he wanted changed. On very important messages, such as the State of the Union, the President might bring in pages of hand-written text to give us the precise wording he wanted on a sensitive point. It was an ideal and very productive relationship. [Orben, p. 20]

CHAPTER III

AUDIENCE ANALYSIS AND
SETTING OBJECTIVES

"Rhetoric finds its end in judgment—for the audience judges the counsels that are given." [Aristotle, *Rhetoric,* Book II, Chapter 1]

S peaking has advantages as a medium of communication that make it highly effective. No other medium allows a message to be tailored to fit its receivers so well. No other medium permits such extensive, immediate feedback.

Exploiting these advantages requires (1) a careful and accurate audience analysis and (2) determination in advance of the desired outcome of the speech.

AUDIENCE ANALYSIS

When a speech writer analyzes an audience, a great deal of stereotyping often takes place. The theory seems to be, "If you've seen one Rotary Club, you've seen 'em all." Sometimes this approach works well, and the speech is a success. Sometimes the approach results in a mediocre speech, a speech that failed to take into account subtle special features of a particular audience. Sometimes the system fails badly and results in a speech that bores the audience or makes it hostile.

The most obvious thing to say about audience analysis, then, is that the odds are in most cases it will not turn up anything startling. The analysis will confirm what the speech writer suspected at the outset. But a thorough audience analysis may be compared to the wearing of a life jacket. You use it, not because you expect to fall out of the boat, but because if you do fall out it could save your life.

GUIDELINES

There are a couple of useful rules to follow in finding out about an audience. First, the writer should gather information from more than one person. The writer's most obvious contact with the host organization will probably be the person in charge of the program. That person's main responsibility usually is to get a speaker to agree to talk. After a speaker accepts, the program chair begins to lose interest in the problem, and the writer may have to pump for information.

Many people may prove more helpful than the program chair. Officers might be expected to know a great deal about their members, but they sometimes give polite or "official" answers which can mislead. The principal of the school, for example, will probably give a more glowing account of the PTA than you would get from a trusted former teacher. Any personal friend of the writer who belongs to the host organization should be willing to help out. A corporation may have sponsored members who can be useful.

For speeches in a distant city, contacts in the press might be able to supply needed facts. And you will have an excellent source if you locate someone who wrote a speech previously given to the group.

A second rule suggests you get some of your data orally. The neat printed forms used by many communication departments to gather audience information can be helpful, but answers tend to be too brief at times. And written answers don't provide the extra insights you get from tone of voice and facial expression. A request for information on educational background may be answered on a form with the words, "Fifty percent have graduate degrees," whereas a conversation over a drink may produce "half the group's a bunch of smart aleck eggheads." Even over the telephone, informers tend to be more informative than they would be in writing.

Usefulness of Data

Some of the knowledge gained about an audience will directly affect the content of the speech. Material you would use before one audience you would not want presented to another audience even though the topic remained the same. A speaker, who apparently pulled an old speech out of the files, once addressed an audience with repeated statements such as "your wives know," "if you ask your wife," and "as your wives will tell you." The audience was overwhelmingly female.

Some facts learned about an audience may be mainly of psychological benefit. If a writer has in mind a clear, sharply focused image of the audience, writing the speech is likely to be a more comfortable process than if the audience is a mental blur to the writer.

The speaker, too, gains a degree of psychological comfort from knowing about the audience. A brief account of information uncovered by the writer about the audience could well accompany an early draft of the speech. The speaker could benefit from something as simple as a sketch showing the meeting room and indicating who will be at the head table.

Occasionally, information the writer gathers will require action at the site of the speech. The lighting may be wrong, for example, or the microphone may require adjustment. In those cases where the writer does not accompany the speaker, the information should be passed on to the appropriate person. In political campaigns, this person would be the "advance agent," the representative of the speaker who has the responsibility for taking care of local arrangements. If no one is assigned this role, perhaps the speaker could be provided with information suggesting the kinds of alterations likely to be needed.

Here are some specific items to be checked (remember that even though the answer usually will be obvious and of routine importance, occasionally vital facts will be turned up):

NAME OF THE GROUP

Be sure to get the group's name exactly right. If the audience is a Jaycee chapter in Gotham City, it may be the West End Chapter or it may be the Southside Chapter, and the two may have a heated rivalry going. The story is perhaps apocryphal, but the writer who prepared a speech for the Handicapped Bowlers League should have written one for the Handicap Bowlers League.

DATE, TIME, AND TRAVEL PLANS

Someone has to make sure which Holiday Inn will be the

site of the speech, whether eight o'clock is a.m. or p.m., and in which year the May 12 speaking date is supposed to fall. It's also useful to know the best combination of air, sea, and land transportation to get a speaker safely on the scene.

THE PHYSICAL SETTING

A speaker once went to a great deal of trouble to arrange to close a curtain that opened onto an attractive swimming pool just to the right rear of the speakers stand. The speaker knew that the appearance of just one muscle-bound beach boy or a single bikini-clad beauty contestant would blot out half the speech. Details of this sort should be checked before every speech.

PODIUM

For example, there should be adequate lighting for the speaker to read by, and there should be no spotlights creating glare that blinds the speaker. The light level on the speaker should be about the same as that on the audience. Distracting flower arrangements, awards trophies, or art work should be out of sight. The background music should be killed before the speeches start.

MEETING ROOM

The speaker or the speaker's aide should always know the name of a responsible hotel or restaurant management person to contact in advance about coordination of such problems as removal of dishes and for emergency help in case of unexpected construction noises or other on-site interference.

For an important speech, someone should make sure no noisy events are to be held in an adjoining room. Attention should be paid to traffic in hallways; if it cannot be diverted, signs should be posted saying "Meeting in Progress" and doors into the meeting room near the speaker should be closed with "Use Other Entrance" signs on them.

PUBLIC ADDRESS SYSTEM AND LECTERN

The microphone should be checked out in advance for quality

and for position. The lectern must be of the proper size and height. Especially for tall or short speakers it may be wise to have a lectern with built-in microphone that travels with the speaker. The head table may not be the best place from which the speech should be given, and the lectern might be set up along the side of the room for best effect. Ira Hayes of NCR gives a popular speech for which he has prepared a diagram showing exactly how the platform should be arranged for his talk.

Head Table

The speaker should know in advance who will be at the head table and what their positions will be. The name of the presiding officer and the person who will give the speech of introduction should be known to the speaker. Knowing about others who might be seated at the front could help the speaker prepare to avoid the plight of a major of New Orleans who dined in a famous seafood restaurant with President Roosevelt. After a long and uncomfortable silence, the mayor finally arrived at the point where he had to say something, so he asked, "Well, Mr. President, how do you like them ersters?"

The speech of introduction presents a special problem. A bad introduction may set the wrong mood and make at least the opening few minutes of a speech quite awkward. The best solution to this problem is to prepare a speech of introduction and send it to the person who is to give it. Such an introduction should be short and simple, and it can be typed so that it resembles an ordinary vita sheet. As a rule, however, no full vita should be sent. Too many speakers have endured the embarrassment of hearing inappropriate items selected out of context or, even worse, having an entire vita of three or four single-spaced pages read word for word. More will be said about speeches of introduction in a later chapter.

Length of the Speech

The standard length of the modern business speech seems to be about fifteen to twenty minutes. Increasingly, speakers are expected to answer questions for perhaps an additional quarter of an hour. So, the speech writer needs to know exactly how much of the time allotted the speaker is to be used for the actual speech. The speaker should be informed not only of the time set aside for the speech and the Q&A but should also be told when the program is to adjourn. A wise speaker will use this information to shorten the Q&A session if the program runs overtime.

NATURE OF THE PROGRAM

Because a speech is not given in a vacuum, a writer needs to learn as much as possible about the nature of the program of which the speech will be a part. The reason for the meeting should be determined to find out if there is some special occasion such as awards night or boss's night. If there is to be a business meeting following the speech, it might be a good idea to see if your speaker can politely leave to avoid spending time in what might prove to be a dull discussion of a club's budget.

OTHER SPEAKERS

No writer should assume any one speech will be the only presentation at a meeting and should make a special effort to find out if other speakers will be present. This information will give a writer the opportunity to relate a topic to other program talks and might avoid an embarrassing situation. A speaker who will be preceded by a moving address on drug addiction might not be able to use the piece of humor you had planned to put in the opening of the talk.

The number of speakers on the program, the length of time the audience has been meeting (is the evening dinner meeting an extension of a full day or week of papers and talks?), and the length of the pre-program open bar are all important to the writer.

UNUSUAL EVENTS

There should be no surprises. A famous news correspondent once watched what he apparently assumed was to be a serious event grow steadily more giddy. The last straw came shortly before the correspondent's speech when someone dressed in an armadillo costume led the entire group in a rather unusual dance. The speaker was forced to throw away his announced text and substitute a much more informal presentation. If the nature of the program had been known, the speaker could have come prepared with an appropriate talk.

On occasion a writer may be in a position to suggest that offbeat program events be altered or cancelled. For example, a gag gift for the speaker that is intended in a spirit of wholesome fun could ruin a speech if it is not known about and kept under control.

PRESS AND PUBLICITY

Extensive media coverage of a speech may actually redefine the audience for the writer. The ultimate target of the talk might be TV viewers and newspaper readers. While this situation does not mean the immediate audience can be ignored, presence of the press might substantially affect the aim and content of the body of the speech.

Some writers believe preparing a press release is the best way to start the speech writing process. They feel a press release puts the central theme of the speech in focus. Other writers, however, take the position that the most newsworthy feature of the speech may not be the most important part of the message.

Another controversy among writers in regard to the press involves the question of when to release the text of a speech. Some regard pre-delivery release as a good idea; others fear this practice cuts down on news coverage. The number of variables to be taken into account in making this decision suggests that no firm rule can be applied. The wisdom of releasing an advance text depends on the circumstances surrounding the speech under consideration.

But both the writer and the speaker should know the extent of press coverage expected. This knowledge will be both of psychological value and useful in planning the tone and substance of the talk.

DEMOGRAPHY

Some audience information the speech writer needs to gather is much like that collected by the census taker. Size of audience, sex make-up, ethnic groups represented, age range, educational data, and occupations of audience members should all be known before beginning to write a speech.

Size. While the size of the audience is hardly likely to affect the subject matter of a speech, it can have an effect on such features as the degree of formality of the language of the talk. Also, a speaker's morale may drop considerably if the speaker expects a huge crowd but in fact only a handful attend. The reverse is also true, the speaker will be protected from shock if warned in advance by the writer that the crowd will be much larger than the speaker is accustomed to addressing.

Sex. In most speeches the ratio of men to women in the audience will make little difference. But in some cases a heavy preponderance of one sex or the other, taken in combination with other facts gathered, may cause a writer to support a point with different illustrations or statistics than otherwise would have been used. For example, an audience made up of ninety percent women could be expected to show more interest in an illustration of manufacturing costs based on women's shoes than on ball bearings. The rule would not hold, of course, if the women were mechanical engineers. Nor would the ball bearing illustration be necessarily wise for an audience of male shoe clerks.

Even if information about sex distribution in the audience were not to affect the material in the speech, it would once again be an example of useful information for the psychological comfort of the speaker. The more clear the speaker's image of audience, the more at ease the speaker is likely to feel.

Ethnic Groups. Many corporations recruit for their speakers bureaus those employees who speak the native language of ethnic groups among the company's customers. While adaptation of a speech to fit an audience does not often call for the use of a language other than English, other more subtle adaptations may be in order. Again remembering that other factors need to be considered in conjunction with ethnic makeup of an audience, the fact that large numbers of Mexican-Americans or French Canadians will be present can significantly change a speech. The American Heart Association has an audience analysis form for speaker bureau members that calls for a check into ethnic backgrounds of audiences. If it is discovered that Blacks will be in attendance, the speaker is instructed to add additional material on high blood pressure supplied by the Association.

Age. Older citizens have been active in recent years in organizing to protect their interests. This movement demonstrates the importance of reaching older listeners and suggests a level of special concerns that writers must examine. Younger audiences are also becoming increasingly sought as speakers attempt to get their messages across to an audience with considerable buying power and with minds not fully made up on some crucial issues.

An analysis of an audience that fails to determine the age range could produce a speech that fails to hold interest or move listeners toward the speaker's point of view.

Education and Occupation. In a typical case of audience analysis, a sketch of listeners' educational backgrounds and their occupations will immediately provide the writer with clues to aid in the construction of a speech.

Before leaving the area of demographic analysis, it might be wise to recall that the era has long passed where information of this sort was gathered merely to know when to avoid racist, sexist, or other offensive types of jokes. Intelligent communication demands a sensitivity to interests of special groups. A writer who is squeamish on this subject might take a look at the number of specialized newspaper columns, limited readership magazines, employee publications, and narrowly targeted radio or TV programs. Fully understanding the concerns of special groups in an audience does not mean a speech should pander to listeners. It means that speeches must take the audience into account if they are not to be boring and irrelevant.

SPECIFIC INDIVIDUALS PRESENT

In addition to learning who will be at the head table, a writer should always ask if there are any other special persons present. A major opponent of the speaker may attend, a harsh critic of the speaker's company or profession may be present, or a personal friend from the speaker's past may be in the audience. The writer can protect a speaker from awkward situations with this kind of information.

Alf Goodykoontz, Executive Editor of the *Richmond Times-*

Dispatch and a popular speaker, makes a habit of mentioning two or three names of members of his audience during a talk. Speech writers can make effective use of the "Goodykoontz Rule." In the case of speaking from manuscript, it obviously is necessary to take some precautions. If the speaker cannot be depended on to check the matter out immediately before the speech, then the reference must be made in a general way. "I'm sure Mayor Snort will be happy to learn of. . . ." will be safer than "Mayor Snort here tonight will be happy to learn of. . . ."

KNOWLEDGE AND OPINION

It is easier to gather descriptions of an audience than it is to get a clear picture of what members of an audience know and think. Yet a speech writer must make some effort to discover an audience's level of knowledge and opinion on the speaker's subject. Extensive conversations with several people who know the audience may be necessary. Reading local publications can help. A writer may attend a meeting a month in advance of a speech to size up the audience.

A writer hopes to avoid extremes. Telling an audience something it knows so well that nothing new can be added is as bad as telling an audience something above its ability to grasp. Also, a ringing speech arguing for a point listeners accepted long ago wastes as much time as a powerful effort to change minds that are completely closed on a subject. Only by understanding what an audience knows and thinks can a writer avoid these dangers.

AUDIENCE ANALYSIS: A CASE HISTORY

In the spring of 1976 Dick Charlton and Kathie Kornack of J I Case gathered material for a Carthage College commencement address to be delivered by Morris W. Reid, Case's Chairman of the Board. The two writers did an outstanding job of audience analysis and adaptation.

They prepared a questionnaire and sent it along with a personal letter from Mr. Reid to every member of the Carthage graduating class. The large number of replies they got gave them an excellent description of the primary audience of the speech.

The students supplied data on their education and their job interests. They revealed their attitudes on economics, politics, families, government versus business careers, and the role of women in society. Nearly half of those responding accepted the invitation to make additional comments.

The writers used the data in three ways. First, on the basis of the students' feelings revealed in the survey, they wrote a speech that reinforced positive attitudes about the country and the economy. Second, they used the replies from the students for much of the content of the speech. The survey was summarized in the middle of the speech, and two student comments were quoted. Third, at the conclusion of the ceremony the graduates were given a compilation of the results of the survey which was printed at the end of a booklet containing the text of the speech they had just heard (in the speech they had been told they would get the results and were asked to save the questions to ask their own children in twenty-five years).

As a final touch in adapting the speech to the audience, each student received a quote taken from the conclusion of the address and encased with a Bicentennial silver dollar. While few occasions will demand or even permit such extensive audience analysis, the principle upon which the writers proceeded has universal application: "Know your audience."

DETERMINING SPEECH OBJECTIVES

A speech writer was sitting in his office late one afternoon when his boss stopped by. "You know that meeting I'm going to next month," the boss said, "Well, they want me to give a speech."

The speech writer reached for pen and paper as he asked, "What about?"

The boss gave his answer over his shoulder as he started out of the office and down the hallway. "About twenty minutes," he said.

The story is factual. And worse than that, it represents an attitude about speech making that is all too common. Many speakers and speech writers regard the primary purpose of a talk as filling an allotted time slot on a program. This is not to say they regard the content as totally unimportant, it's just that they see the aim of the speech as honoring a request. Beyond a vague expectation that the speaker and perhaps the speaker's organization will gain a little gratitude, such writers and speakers think little about the matter of determining speech objectives.

While any speech writer may be required some day to write a "throw away" speech, a professional writer should be constantly aware of the possible impact of a speech. That impact can be stated simply: Every speech should be designed to change an audience.

At the beginning of every writing assignment, then, a writer should ask, "How do I expect *this* audience to be changed by *this* speech?" That question should be periodically reviewed as the writing progresses.

The kinds of change that can be brought about must be considered systematically. It is not enough, as Professor William Norwood Brigance once noted, to change an audience so that it is numb on one end and dumb on the other.

SPECIFIC AUDIENCE CHANGES

Figure 2 depicts four changes a speech might bring about. The changes are shown in a stairstep diagram for two reasons. First, from bottom to top each change is progressively harder to achieve, and, second, each step builds on the one before.

To INFORM

Although the transfer of information is by no means simple, relatively speaking it is the simplest and easiest change to bring about in an audience. The results of such a speech are judged by the amount of information the audience learned or the new insights gained in respect to information already known. Teaching and training are two areas where information transfer is frequently found, but often government or business may need to play the teaching role.

Example. To illustrate the various changes on the stairsteps, an example will be offered for each one. Two factors will be kept constant: the speaker and the subject. The speaker in the examples will be the Vice President of a utility company, and the subject will be "Our New Marketing Plan." The variables

Fig. 2

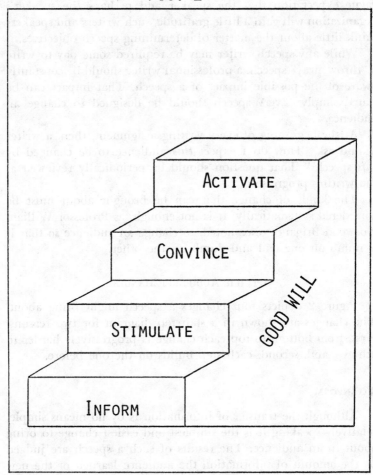

Speech Purposes

will be those facts commonly gathered in an audience analysis, the facts that tell the writer which purposes are realistic and which are not.

Our informative speech will be given to company employees. They have heard rumors of a new, aggressive marketing approach under consideration by top management, but no details have been released. Through careful inquiry the speech writer has found no opposition to the new idea exists among employees, but neither are they strongly for the plan. The speech writer urged that this speech be given before word of the change reached the general public. The talk will be given to a half dozen employee groups over a period of two days. It will tell why the company abandoned its old policy, how the new one will work, and what the company expects to gain.

To Stimulate

The speech to stimulate might be called a pep talk. It takes an idea the audience approves of and reminds them, not merely what they believe, but why they believe and why it is good that they believe. The old-fashioned Fourth-of-July Oration in the United States is a good example of the speech to stimulate. But the speech of stimulation is by no means dead. Politicians still use it in addressing their supporters. Business executives of like mind often meet to hear one of their number damn their enemies and praise their friends. At graduation exercises, retirement banquets, and building dedications the speech to stimulate serves a useful purpose.

Example. The Vice President of the utility company has been invited to give an address at the annual luncheon for company speaker bureau members. The company marketing plan has been in effect for a year now, and the speakers bureau has been used as one means to sell the idea to the public. The speech writer has discovered that the members of the bureau are themselves sold on the plan, and they are proud of their presentations on the subject. The writer has included in the talk specific facts about the speeches given by members of the bureau, and the Vice President will spend twenty minutes telling them what a good job they have done and how much the company appreciates their help.

To Convince

Understanding the nature of the speech to convince starts with the recognition that there must be a specific issue at stake. The writer should be able to state the issue in the form of a proposition written out as a single complete sentence. The proposition should be one the speaker believes, but one the target audience either opposes or has not yet formed an opinion on. Propositions may be of three types.

Fact. First is the proposition of fact. In this case, the audience does not accept a factual statement as true. The difference between the speech to inform and the speech to convince on a proposition of fact is little more than the presence or absence of a conviction in the listener's mind. "We have a new marketing policy" is a factual statement not likely to be disbelieved. On the other hand, a speaker who argues, "We are not guilty of any of the twelve safety violations alleged in the newspapers" may be stating a fact very much in doubt.

Policy. A proposition of policy contends something should or should not be done. As in all the speeches to convince, the writer should have reason to assume the audience disagrees with the proposition or has no opinion. The speech to convince on a proposition of policy does not call for any action on the part of listeners; for the speech to be successful the audience at the end of the speech must simply believe in the soundness of the speaker's view. Speeches arguing "property taxes should be lower" or "environmental safeguards should be stronger" are examples of propositions of policy.

Value. A proposition of value contends that something is good or bad. A speech proclaiming the virtues of the free enterprise system, which would be a speech to stimulate if given to believers, would be a speech to convince if delivered before a dubious audience.

Example. The convincing speech by the utility company Vice President of Marketing is delivered to a group of journalism students. The writer's research has determined that a large majority of the students believe utility companies should not promote their services. Conversations with several of the students and one professor have led the writer to believe the students are not firm in their beliefs but simply do not know much about the subject and have not heard an articulate presentation for the opposite view.

To Actuate

The speech to actuate aims for the audience to take action. Obviously a speech to convince may imply an action. For example, if the audience in an illustration cited above is convinced property taxes should be lower, listeners might logically be expected to vote for changes or sign petitions to get the issue on the ballot. But in the speech to actuate, the call to action will be explicit in the speech and the action will follow almost immediately after the speech. If three characteristics are present, the likelihood that a speech will result in action is increased.

Clear. The desired action should be clearly specified. Many speakers who would like to see something done about the issues they discuss fail to tell the audience what to do. Often this failure seems to result from timidity. The speaker dances to the edge of the cliff and then pulls back quickly to avoid taking the plunge. In some cases the problem simply has not been carefully thought through, and the speaker doesn't have a clear idea of what the audience can or ought to do.

An audience can take only a fairly limited number of actions. They can give, volunteer, sign a petition, write an elected representative, form a committee, and not a great deal more. Whatever the action is, the speaker should set it forth clearly. "So, then, tonight I urge you to join other civic groups throughout the city in voting to endorse the resolution. I hope to be able to report to the committee that your vote was unanimous."

Easy. The action should be made easy for an audience. This may require some extra-rhetorical devices. If a resolution is to be voted on, copies of it ought to be available. If money is to be collected, pledge cards and envelopes should be distributed. If letters are to be written, the proper mailing addresses and titles should be provided along with a fact sheet on the issue (but not a form letter).

Necessary. The speech to get action should establish a clear connection between the belief the speech has instilled or reawakened and the action that should result. The revival preacher who has the choir sing "one more verse" knows there is a convinced sinner in the congregation who hasn't quite yet translated belief into action. The speaker who wants action should end strongly and stress the need for the recommended action.

Example. To examine an action speech by the utility company Vice President, the clock must be turned back to the day the company board met to vote on the proposed plan. The speech writer had found out that over half the board had no conviction one way or the other on the plan. Twenty-five percent were mildly for the plan; the remaining twenty-five percent were against it. The opposition was found to spring mainly from caution, with only two of the opponents feeling strongly on the matter. The writer decided that success stories from other utilities would provide the most compelling evidence for the plan, and a great deal of information was gathered to show what other companies were doing. Attractive visuals were prepared to show anticipated growth in profit, and an easy-to-read summary of the plan was distributed as a handout at the end of the formal presentation.

FEATURES OF THE STAIRSTEP MODEL

As was noted earlier, the speech objectives on the stairstep model are cumulative and are of progressive difficulty.

Cumulative. Each of the purposes builds on the lower one. A speech to stimulate must inform, a speech to convince both informs and stimulates, and a speech to actuate incorporates all the other purposes. The point to keep in mind, however, is that the speech writer must be concerned only with the ultimate purpose of the speech. Therefore, the intended effect of the speech should always be stated as one word. The effect is to inform or stimulate or convince or actuate. To use the word "and" is to diffuse the focus of the speech. A writer need not plan a speech to "inform and convince" because a speech to convince necessarily informs in the process of achieving its ultimate goal.

The notion of cumulative effect rests on a crucial assumption. It assumes a homogenous audience. This assumption must be checked in preparing each speech, but fortunately it will frequently hold. Audiences, after all, tend to come together because they have something in common. When the assumption does not hold, the writer may decide essentially to ignore one segment of the audience and aim the message at another segment. In one case diehard opposition may be written off to direct a speech at neutrals in the audience, while in another case partisans of the speaker's cause can be disregarded to use the speech to reach the unconverted.

The stairstep model suggests an underpinning of good will should result from any speech as an automatic by-product. We live in a polite society, and audiences appreciate the effort demonstrated in a good speech. In spite of the humor that abounds about dull speeches, a speaker who does a credible job will collect a measure of appreciation from most audiences.

Degrees of Difficulty. Exceptions will occur, but generally the purposes described above are presented in an order of increasing difficulty. Speakers make two errors in failing to understand the varied difficulty of speech objectives. In some cases, speakers try to go too far. A speech trying to convince the alarmed members of a homeowners association that a chemical waste dump in their neighborhood is a wonderful idea will almost surely fail. If there is any point in speaking to such a group at all, the speech would have to be a carefully arranged effort to describe the facts in the case. On the other hand—and this is a far more common problem—speakers go before friendly audiences without daring to do more than belt out another speech designed to stimulate. In many cases a talk to support a specific policy or a speech to get action would make better use of the speaker's time and the audience's ability to contribute to a cause.

The speech writer should examine the stairstep figure with the intent of climbing as high in a given speech as possible. The more ambitious the goal, the more return the writer will get on the investment of time and energy in preparing a speech.

ACCEPTING SPEAKING ENGAGEMENTS

Some speeches should never be given. And the speech writer should have a say in the setting up of a policy on accepting engagements. The writer may know better than anyone else when an engagement promises to be a no-win situation. When none of the objectives discussed in this chapter appears feasible or when none of them appears worth the effort, the engagement should be declined.

SPEAKING TO ENTERTAIN

The speech designed to entertain has not been considered in the discussion so far. Because the objective of that type of speech is so unlike the others, it will be dealt with in the chapter on speeches for special occasions.

CONCLUSION

Professor Donald Bryant has defined public speaking as a process in which ideas are adjusted to people and people are adjusted to ideas. That definition is at the heart of the matter of audience analysis and setting objectives. The audience must be studied with care to learn what it can accept and how the material must be presented to fit the needs, interests, and abilities of the audience. Then the writer must decide how the audience itself is to be "adjusted" by picking the objective the speech should have.

The model described in this chapter is an abstraction. There are times when the real world does not fit the model precisely. But the model often works smoothly, and it always keeps before the writer the rule that a speech should be designed to bring about a change in an audience.

CHAPTER IV

ORGANIZATION OF IDEAS

*"First, I tell them what I'm going to tell them. Then I tell
them. And then I tell them what I've told them."* [A
classic formula for organizing a sermon]

A long with all its advantages as a medium of communication,
speech has one major disadvantage. It is instantaneous. The
message must be grasped at the moment it is uttered or the
listener fails to get the point. Speech does not allow a listener
the privilege a reader has to put a book down and think about
an idea or even to go back and reread a passage.

It follows, then, that speeches must be organized with particular care to make it easy for a listener to follow the speaker's
thinking. The structure of a speech is not necessarily more rigid
or logical than that of, for instance, a report. But the structure
must take the needs of the listener into account.

There is no one perfect formula for organizing a speech.
Writers use a variety of methods, but only one system will be
discussed in detail here. It is based on the same principles found
in any well-organized speech, and it is a highly flexible formula
that will avoid making all speeches sound the same.

The formula has four parts:

I. The Opening

II. The Thesis Statement

III. The Body (with two to five main points)
A. Main Point
B. Main Point
C. Main Point

IV. The Close

THE OPENING

The opening of a speech ordinarily consists of a minute or

two of material designed to (1) get the attention and interest of the audience, (2) get the audience in a friendly mood, and (3) begin to orient the audience to the speaker's subject. In some instances all three of the initial goals may be accomplished at once. A speaker who opens with "I'm here to tell you how you can all get rich" might instantly have an attentive, friendly, well-oriented audience. But each goal is distinct, and more than a single statement is usually necessary. Obviously an audience may be attentive without being in a good mood or it may be well-oriented but uninterested.

A number of proven techniques can be drawn upon to make sure all the goals are accomplished. These techniques form a sort of recipe for preparing a good opening. The instructions are flexible but simple: mix in enough of the techniques to accomplish the required goals for a particular audience.

At the outset of the discussion of techniques for opening a speech, the social nature of speech making should be noted. Writers generally prepare speeches in a formal setting. Writing speeches is work. Piles of facts and figures may be on the desk. The writer is probably in a somber mood. But, while the degree of formality may vary from speech to speech, speeches are not usually given in a thoroughly business atmosphere. Food (and drink) may be consumed. The speech is often delivered after working hours have ended. A large number of people are sitting close together and in all likelihood have been talking to one another before the speech. While they are prepared for the speaker to be serious, they are also prepared for the speaker to be social.

THE COMMON BOND

The common bond, which frequently helps open channels of communication in social situations, consists of bringing up some point of interest shared by the speaker and the audience. It may be as important as a mutual dedication to a noble cause or as casual as a common interest in the local football team.

Observing conversations between strangers at parties will reveal how effectively the common bond works in helping establish a friendly relationship or create interest. In such situations people discuss the common ground they find in their jobs, hobbies, or problems. One frequent conversational opener using the common ground approach is the "Do you know so-and-so?" gambit. Discovering a mutual friend is often enough to validate one speaker to another.

THE HONEST COMPLIMENT

Almost anyone's interest is perked up by a sincere compliment. And we generally develop a quite friendly attitude toward those who say nice things about us. The key to using this approach in a speech, of course, is to find something the speaker genuinely appreciates about the audience. "It's nice to be back in my favorite city" needs to be said with true feeling if it is to be accepted.

As was true in the case of the common bond, the compliment is a powerful force in social situations. A heartfelt expression of commendation can spur a fellow worker on to greater success or even provide a discouraged spouse with incentive to help keep a marriage afloat.

HUMOR

The old practice of starting every speech with two or three hoary jokes has just about ended among successful speakers. But humor still has a place in gaining attention and winning good will from an audience at the opening of a speech. Humor will be discussed more fully in a separate chapter, but for now it should be noted that except for speakers who are skilled in handling humor, a low-key, low-risk approach is best. There is a simple test for low-risk humor. If the audience does not laugh, will the content of the comment be strong enough in its own right to avoid embarrassment to the speaker? If the answer is yes, the material can stay in whether it gets a laugh or not.

When low-risk humor elicits an audience response, it should be considered successful even when that response is only a smile or a chuckle. The purpose of humor in a speech, whether in the opening or elsewhere, is not to get laughter as an end in itself. Humor builds a friendly climate, attracts and holds attention, and should illuminate a point the speaker is making. Thus, humor can be useful in achieving all three of the goals of a speech opening.

THE OPENING ILLUSTRATION

Starting a speech with an illustration can be a powerful way to get an audience's attention. An illustration is a story with a built-in curiosity factor; most listeners will stay tuned in to see how it turns out. An opening story is highly flexible. Many writers assume a beginning story must be humorous or at least light. It can be, but as the opening of Lester Pearson's Nobel Peace Prize Acceptance Address of 1957 shows, it does not have to be:

> I remember one poignant illustration of the futility and tragedy of war. It was concerned . . . with civilian destruction in London in 1941 during its ordeal by bombing. It was a quiet Sunday morning after a shattering night of fire and death. I was walking past the smoking ruins of houses that had been bombed and burned during the night. The day before they had been a neat row of humble, red brick workingmen's dwellings. They were now rubble except for the front wall of one building which may have been some kind of community club and on which there was a plaque that read "Sacred to the memory of the men of Alice Street who died for peace during the Great War, 1914-1918." The children and grand-children of those men of Alice Street had now in their turn been sacrificed in the Greater War, 1939-1945. For Peace? There are times when it does not seem so.

The illustration can be taken from personal experience, as seen in Pearson's opening, or it can be borrowed. Sometimes a hypothetical illustration can be constructed; the drama of the story can be captured even if it is obviously imaginary.

REFERENCE TO THE SUBJECT

Most audiences are not ready to hear the substance of what a speaker has to say in the opening of a speech. Listeners at that point are still getting settled in their chairs, finishing a cup of coffee, or adjusting to the sight and sound of the speaker. Only rarely, then, can a speaker use a reference to the subject as the very first device in an opening.

Here is the opening line of a manuscript which probably did not make an audience gasp with excitement: "Recently some federal regulations were changed which affect the way telephone service is provided. They are important changes, and I want to tell you about them." When members of the audience discovered later in the speech that the important changes made possible a credit of sixty-five cents a month on their bills, they were no doubt still not totally entranced.

Reference to the subject, however, provides an excellent way to get an audience oriented. It can provide a transition from the rest of opening to the thesis statement of the speech. It can even be used in the opening few seconds if the topic is one in which the audience is intensely interested.

Alternatives. In addition to the five major techniques for opening a speech, a number of seldom-used approaches might be considered. A speech can begin with a startling statement, for example, or with a rhetorical question. If a writer is not careful, these methods may appear to demand rather than to deserve attention. The same criticism can be made against the speaker who opens with a gimmick. Obviously it takes a skillful speaker to capitalize on the attention gained from starting a speech on litter by dumping a bag of roadside trash on the floor in front of the startled audience.

CASE HISTORY: OPENING TECHNIQUES

John W. Hanley, Chairman and President of Monsanto, makes effective use of the five techniques described. His speech openings are always tailored to fit each audience he addresses because he consistently finds a fresh and lively way to apply the techniques. A sample Hanley opening appears below. It is from a speech delivered before the Town Hall of California in Los Angeles on June 14, 1977. A quick glance at the passage will show that it makes use of all five of the techniques.

This year marks an anniversary of sorts for me in Los Angeles. Exactly thirty years ago, I came here to start my career as a soap salesman. Five days after I arrived, I met a lovely young Beverly Hills girl, and within a few months she was, somewhat shyly, selling soap and helping me win a sales contest. For the 29 years since, as Mrs. Hanley, she has been my confidante and co-worker.

So, as you can see, I have reason for fond memories of this city and its people.

I want to thank all of you for taking certain risks to come here this afternoon. Let me hasten to add I don't mean, by this, to disparage your wonderful freeways. But whether you drove—with or

without seatbelts—or whether you simply walked across a street or
two, there were in fact some risks involved.

I don't say this facetiously. It's an unfortunate fact that there
is an element of risk in everything we do. And it is with a keen
awareness of this fact that I chose as my topic, "Why Ban Reason
From The Consumer Safety Debate?"

Frankly, I have become increasingly concerned about what seems
to me an atmosphere of crisis and hysteria surrounding consumer
safety. The debate over what is safe, and what regulations are
needed to enforce safety, is growing daily in volume and intensity,
but regrettably, not in reasonableness and rationality. This year is
shaping up as the biggest ever for wholesale banishment of suspect
goods from the marketplace. The saccharin case is likely to be a
forerunner of a series of potential future decisions about the market-
ability of food products.

I'm grateful to have this opportunity to contribute another perspective on this subject—and to do so before Town Hall, which has
a richly deserved reputation for its steadfast commitment to public
dialogue as an instrument for setting future directions for our nation.

I want to speak today about the role you and I can play in
putting reason back into the consumer safety debate.

ANALYSIS

A brief review of Hanley's techniques may prove useful. In
Paragraph No. 1 an illustration and a common bond are combined. A compliment appears in Paragraph No. 2. Paragraphs
No. 3, No. 4, and No. 5 refer to the subject with a slight touch
of humor. Paragraph No. 6 once again compliments the
audience, and Paragraph No. 7 sets forth the thesis of the speech.

This opening, which lasts for about two minutes, can reasonably be expected to have made the audience attentive, friendly,
and aware of the speaker's theme. The illustration in Paragraph
No. 1 has an element of drama in it, and at the same time it
manages indirectly to commend the audience for its fine city. By
the time the speaker reaches Paragraph No. 6, the use of the
compliment is direct and straightforward. The use of humor in
Paragraph No. 3 is low-key, and the reference to the subject
in Paragraphs No. 3, No. 4, and No. 5 comes only after all four
of the other techniques have already been used.

THE THESIS STATEMENT

After the opening of the speech, the next step is to state

the theme of the talk in a simple sentence or two. The final
paragraph quoted from the Hanley talk illustrates this segment
of a speech. It should make clear to the audience exactly what
the speech is to cover.

Some writers extend the thesis statement, the "tell them
what you are going to tell them" section of the talk, to include
an outline of the main points. Mr. Robert F. Dee, Chairman of
the Board and CEO of Smithkline Corporation, used this approach in a speech to a conference on innovation. In unmistak-
ably clear terms, Dee said, "I would like to cover three points.
The first deals with the meaning of innovation. The second with
the environment in which it can be expected to flourish. And the
third with the state of innovation in the United States today."
[Dee, pp. 2-3]

THE BODY OF THE SPEECH

In the body of the speech, the writer should develop two to
five main ideas to support the thesis statement. Ideally, the
audience should know at any time during the speech exactly
which point is being developed, and at the end of the speech
the audience should know how many points were presented as
well as the ideas the points expressed.

PATTERNS

When a writer begins to put together the body of a speech,
the material needed will ordinarily be scattered about. One fact
will be in a report, another in a magazine article, yet another in
the writer's notes. This random material must somehow be put
in order.

The concept of main points provides a means for an intelligent grouping of data. The concept rests on the assumption
that mere facts do not speak for themselves; they must be used
to support "points" or claims the speaker wishes to establish. The
initial task of the writer, then, is to arrive at a limited number
of points to be developed in support of the thesis of the speech.
One approach to this task calls for the writer to experiment
with various patterns to see which pattern offers the best arrangement of points.

Time. The facts in the speech may be rationally grouped in a chronological sequence. Probably the most commonly seen time pattern is the three point speech dealing with past, present, and future. With such an arrangement the writer has a logical point under which each item of information fits (even though some pieces of data may, depending on how they are used, work in two or more points equally well).

Irving Shapiro, Chairman of Du Pont, used time order in a speech called "The Lawyer's Special Role." [*Vital Speeches,* February 15, 1979, pp. 258-61] He discussed the lawyer's role first "through some history" and used the second half of the speech to consider the role of "the lawyer today." Shapiro, a lawyer himself, developed his first point by explaining the historic images of the lawyer and in his second point made several suggestions to guide the conduct of modern lawyers.

Space. Points may sometimes be produced by grouping facts according to space or geography. This system makes ideas especially easy for an audience to visualize and keep in order. The clarity of ideas presented in space order may be seen in a telephone industry speech of a few years ago. The thesis of the speech was "To explain the long distance telephone network." The first point discussed long distance telephone communication by land and the second point dealt with transmission by undersea cable. It is easy to see that many members of an audience would have found the third point a natural extension of the first two: long distance communication through the air by satellite.

In a speech evaluating the problems of the transfer of United States technology, W. S. Anderson, Chairman of NCR, employed two main points built on a geographical distinction. He first considered problems of technology transfer from West to East, the free world to the communist block, and then turned his attention to technology transfer from North to South, the developed to the so-called developing nations. Once again the ideas in a speech on a complex topic were made easy to follow. [Anderson, pp. 1-13]

Topical. By far the most common pattern of main points in speeches is a division based on breaking a subject down into its logical or natural topics. In the speech on technology transfer just mentioned, the speaker might have chosen to substitute for the spatial points a set of points organized around topics such as (1) economic implications of technology transfer, (2) political implications, and (3) military implications. Among the possible topics Mr. Shapiro might have used to discuss the role of the lawyer would be (1) the role of the lawyer as advisor and (2) the role of the lawyer as advocate.

David Rockefeller, Chairman of Chase Manhattan Bank, found the topical division of ideas a good way to examine "The Chief Executive in the Year 2000," a speech he delivered to the Commonwealth Club of California. [*Vital Speeches,* January 1, 1980, pp. 162-64] Here is how Rockefeller previewed his three topical points:

> This afternoon, I'd like to take a first step [toward planning for the future] by covering three areas. First, elaborate a bit more on why I think it's critical that you and I start paving the way for the development of the managers of the next century. Second, discuss several of the environmental challenges that those managers might face, and third, offer a brief "character sketch" of the manner of man or woman I think will be effective in what promises to be a brave, new corporate world.

For another example, John Hanley's "Lessons I've Learned Since Graduation" has three topical points. [*Vital Speeches,* July 15, 1981, pp. 598-600] Here is how the points appear, not in the preview, but in the body of the speech: "Lesson No. 1: Cultivate your curiosity," "This brings me to Lesson No. 2: Enlarge your enthusiasm," and "That's Lesson No. 3: Make the law of averages work for you."

Problem-Solution. It has been suggested above that the number of points developed from the patterns discussed so far should be limited in number to somewhere between two and five. If the problem-solution pattern is used, the nature of the pattern limits the number of points to two.

In his speech, "The U. S. Tire Industry in the 1980's," John D. Ong, Chairman of the BFGoodrich Company, uses the problem-solution pattern to explore difficulties faced by the tire industry and then to attack a much-discussed answer that Ong does not believe will work. [*Vital Speeches,* December 1, 1980, pp. 112-14] Here is his thesis sentence: "Let's examine the problem and then return to this so-called solution."

Raymond C. Tower, President and Chief Operating Officer of FMC, divides his main points into a problem and a solution in the talk, "Government Regulation: Slow Death for Free Enterprise." [*Vital Speeches,* September 1, 1980, pp. 676-80] He sets up his first point by saying, "Let's look at the nature of the attack on the free enterprise system," and introduces his second point with the question, "Well, what can be done to turn back the regulatory tide?"

Using the Patterns Creatively

Any one of the four patterns can be used to write a dull speech. Having three clear points in topical order does little for a speech if it lacks substance. And writers want to avoid falling into a rut by making each successive speech fit a repetitive pattern that may not always set off the speaker's ideas to best advantage.

But the patterns can be used creatively. Look at the variety possible with a single topic. A speech on the environment, for example, might significantly aid an audience's understanding if it presents, in chronological order, an insightful analysis of the eras through which our concern for the environment has passed. A fresh view of the situation might emerge from a speech looking at the environment from a geographic perspective. A great variety of topical divisions are possible. These could range from the obvious air, water, and noise trio to a highly sophisticated presentation of aesthetic, economic, and social perspectives.

A speech need not exhaust every conceivable feature of a subject. A speaker has the right to carve out an announced segment of an issue and deal with that segment alone. Toying with various possible patterns will make available to a writer a healthy number of choices. Far from getting a writer into a repetitious rut, experimentation with the patterns will often suggest new and exciting ideas. The organizational process can and should be a creative one.

Making Main Points Stand Out

As has been stated, by having a clearly delineated set of main points a writer seeks to aid an audience in following the points and even in being able to recall them at the end of a speech. To reach this goal, the discovery of a logical, workable order of ideas is only a first step. The writer must also make sure the points emerge forcefully in the speech.

Not all speeches, not even all good speeches, leave the audience with the points clearly in mind. Usually a good speech without clear main points of the sort being discussed here will nonetheless be logically organized. Lincoln's "Gettysburg Address" certainly does not have three clear main points. However, the most cursory reading of the speech reveals a sound structure in chronological order moving from past (Forescore and seven years ago) to present (the longest section, "Now we are engaged") and future (this nation, under God shall have a new birth of freedom. . . .).

Any writer should have the ability to drive home a set of points in a speech when necessary. Of course, in some speeches clear main points may not be required for success and the division of ideas may hardly be noticed. Such a speech should be the result of a conscious decision on the part of the writer and should not occur simply because the writer did not know how to make major ideas stand out sharply.

Following a few simple guidelines will improve the chances that the main points of a speech will be retained by the audience. The guidelines are listed in order of importance. The tone of the list is prescriptive on the assumption that the writer using it has made the decision to stress main points.

GUIDELINES

Don't Dawdle. Many writers begin the body of a speech hesitantly. Often after a ringing thesis statement of the let-me-tell-you-how-to-save-the-world sort, these writers suddenly get cold feet. The next statement, instead of boldly announcing the first step in saving the world, says something like, "But before we go further, we need to explore the history of the subject." Usually such a tentative, toe-in-the-water start is little more than a stall. Whatever material may be useful in the stalling segment can be plucked out and placed either in the opening or in one of the main points.

Label the Points. No simpler way can be found to identify points clearly than to number them. First, second, and third or number one, number two, and number three will do the job nicely. Variations, such as Hanley's "Lesson No. 1" and "Lesson No. 2" mentioned earlier, are acceptable so long as they are not so subtle that the audience misses the idea.

State the Point. Each point should be stated in a succinct sentence. The points in the Rockefeller speech cited earlier are a bit wordy. Hanley's example is better. Not counting his numbers, Hanley used fourteen words to make three points. Each point expressed a clear idea in a complete sentence.

When a preview is used, writers are reluctant to state the first point because it comes so soon after being mentioned in the preview. They fear, apparently, that they will appear simplistic. That risk is small and the greater fault is not to be understood. Here's how a thesis with a preview and a first point ought to look: "So today I offer you my three keys to getting ahead. Work hard, learn from mistakes, and never cheat. Let's look at that first key, work hard."

Use Previews and Summaries. The preview as part of the thesis statement has already been discussed. The examples presented are quite straightforward, but a preview does not have to be mechanical by any means. Consider the thesis and preview found in the Pearson Nobel Prize Address, an address the speaker entitled, "The Four Faces of Peace." Pearson said, "Our problem then, so easy to state; so hard to solve—is how to bring about a creative peace and a security which will have a strong foundation. . . . I wish to look at the problem in four of its aspects— my 'four faces of peace.' There is Peace and Trade, Peace and Power, Peace and Policy, or Diplomacy [and] Peace and People."

A summary may occur in the conclusion of the speech, a point to be examined later. A useful application of the summary in the body of the speech, however, calls for a recapitulation of ideas perhaps half or two-thirds the way through. "What have we seen so far?" the speaker asks, and then quickly summarizes points A, B, and C before moving on to D and E.

Add Transitions. The speech writer, and sometimes the speaker, gets to know a speech manuscript so well it is easy to forget how complex the ideas will be to an audience. Supplying transitions from one idea to another is a great way to help a listener keep up. The transitions can be simple. Samples might include: "But let us consider another matter" or "Moving on now" or "Turning to an even more pressing issue." Transitions have their place in both writing and speaking, but they are especially needed in speaking.

Parallel Phrasing. Using parallel sentence structure for main points will make them stand out. "The first step in saving the world is. . ." and "The Second step in saving the world is. . ." illustrate this approach.

Other Devices. Writers may resort to having the first letters of key words in each point spell out a word, or they may attempt to have the audience associate each point with some visual image. Rhyming words may be chosen to make the points. Any of these devices must be used with care to avoid letting the technique overshadow or even distort the message.

THE CONCLUSION OF THE SPEECH

Conclusions should be short. When an audience detects a tone of voice suggesting the speech is about to end, the speaker can expect to be listened to for perhaps thirty seconds to a minute. An ending that drags on can undo much of the positive impression of an otherwise good speech.

Conclusions should not end with the all too common "thank you." In the first place, the audience thanks the speaker at the end of a talk, not the other way around. In the second place, should there be some unusual reason for a speaker to be the one to express appreciation, two words would hardly do it. A good statement of thanks would take at least a sentence or two. Speakers use "thank you" as a cop out. They don't trust the ending of the speech and they, in effect, wave a sign saying "That's all, folks." In the process, they miss the opportunity to end on a substantive note or they destroy the effect of any good ending that might have been written in prior to the artificial "thank you."

WAYS TO END A SPEECH

Summary. A summary in the form of a restatement of main

points or by repeating the thesis can be a valuable means of getting the message of the speech concisely before the audience at the conclusion of a speech.

Quotation. A well-stated sentiment which captures the essence of the speech can provide a solid ending. David Mahoney, Chairman and CEO of Norton Simon, ended a speech before the American Association of Advertising Agencies by making a quotation part of his conclusion: "I have one more thought that will put my remarks in perspective. It's a quote from Malcolm Muggeridge, the British writer and social critic, who once said, 'There is no such thing as darkness; only the failure to see.' We in the business community are playing not to lose, instead of playing to win. Let's play to win." [*Vital Speeches,* July 1, 1978, pp. 546-48]

Challenge. In the close of Mr. Mahoney's speech just quoted, the two sentences following his quote offer a good example of a challenge to an audience as part of the conclusion of a speech. Patrick Henry's "Give me liberty or give me death" may be the best known, but the device is still widely used. Here are a number of final sentences taken from speeches in just one issue of *Vital Speeches* [August 15, 1981]: "May we all rise to the challenge ahead." "Harvest a new era in agriculture . . . with more production and less consumption." "Let us get back to the basic job of making America America again—this time for everyone!" "You can count on it!" and "Let's do it!"

Illustration. Just as a story may be used to start a speech, it may be used to end one. Writers sometimes overlook this highly effective way to bring a speech to a close. Mr. Edward Crutchfield, President of the First Union Bank of Charlotte, North Carolina, demonstrated how a story can provide a concise, effective ending.

[L]et me leave you with a hard lesson learned many years ago. I played a little football once for Davidson—a small men's college about 20 miles north of Charlotte. One particularly memorable game for me was one in which I was blindsided on an off-tackle trap. Even though that was 17 years ago, I can still recall the sound of crackling bones ringing in my ears. Well, 17 years and three operations later my back is fine. But, I learned something important about competition that day. Don't always assume that your competition is straight in front of you. It's easy enough to be blindsided

by a competitor who comes at you from a very different direction.
[*Vital Speeches,* June 15, 1980, p. 537]

RHYTHM OF THE CONCLUSION

The final line of a good conclusion to a speech should have a definite beat in the rhythm of the words. It should be read aloud in an early draft to make sure the pulse is right. An example of an irregular beat that produces a weak ending can be seen by simply removing two words from Patrick Henry's famous conclusion. "Give me liberty or death" keeps all the ideas, but it has lost its rhythm.

OTHER WAYS TO STRUCTURE SPEECHES

As already noted, there is not a single best way to organize speeches. The system described above is a good way. It might be discarded, however, in favor of other methods. Two of those deserve brief mention.

THE ONE-POINT SPEECH

Some speeches develop a simple idea that does not need to be broken down into main points. The thesis statement in effect becomes the one and only point in the speech. Mother Teresa, for example, once gave a major address with the theme "smile at one another." The entire speech consisted of stories illustrating the need for love and compassion in the world. [*Vital Speeches,* June 1, 1980, pp. 510-12]

MONROE'S MOTIVATED SEQUENCE

The late Professor Alan Monroe of Purdue University many years ago devised a method of organizing speeches based on what he believed to be the process most of us use in reasoning through a problem. Often recommended for persuasive speeches (to convince or to actuate), the system produces a speech with five parts. [Ehninger, pp. 245-63]

Attention Phase. The first part of Monroe's plan for organizing speeches is much like the opening already discussed. Using any of the techniques presented, the writer must get the attention of the audience.

Need. The need phase of the system can be compared to the problem point in a problem-solution speech. The audience must be shown a need to change something.

Plan. Next, the speech sets forth a solution to the problem. The audience is told what should be believed or what should be done.

Visualization. In the visualization phase of the Monroe pattern the writer gets the audience to see how the solution will work. Or, the writer may choose to show the negative side of the picture and dwell on a vivid accounting of how bad things will look if the solution proposed is not accepted.

Action. In the final phase of the speech, the audience is given a course of action. Listeners are told how to go about implementing the plan.

CONCLUSION

The vast majority of modern speeches do not measure up to the standards of organization proposed here. Often ideas are not written in a logical order, and even when they are, speakers frequently fail to make ideas emerge forcefully enough to be grasped by their listeners. But if a speech is to have its maximum impact on an audience, the members of that audience first of all must be able to follow a speaker's points. The speech writer's aim, then, should be to copy the best organizational features of contemporary speeches and ignore the rest.

Whatever the state of current speaking, our society still prizes logical analysis and clarity of thought. A sound organizational pattern will impress an audience and make a speech writer's job a lot simpler.

CHAPTER V

SUPPORT FOR IDEAS

"What was the speech about?"
"I don't know. The speaker never did say."

There is a popular radio preacher who speaks with a sense of urgency in a commanding voice. He poses questions of great magnitude and can keep an audience spellbound for a quarter of an hour. But he never says anything. Apart from his powerful delivery, his secret seems to be that he allows his listeners to translate his vague generalizations to fit whatever theological views they happen to hold.

IDENTIFICATION OF CLAIMS

Few speakers can get away with that trick, and none should try. If a speaker decides to expend the resources necessary to give a speech, it ought to have something to say. That "something to say" should be subjected to two questions as the speech is being prepared. First, what claim or claims does the speech advance, and second, what evidence can be produced to back up any claim being made?

Let's look first at the notion of a "claim." There's nothing wrong with a speech expressing an opinion or making an assertion. That's essentially what a claim is. The speaker regards the claim as important and wants the audience to think of it the same way.

The place to begin the search for claims is in the thesis statement of a talk. A speaker says, "So I want to explain how government regulation strangles economic growth" or "If the Widget industry is to survive, we must increase productivity" or "Television is poisoning the minds of our youth."

IMPLIED CLAIMS

In a surprising number of cases, speakers imply rather than express the claims they make. All of the claims just cited might well appear in camouflage: "Let's take a look at the significant relationship between government regulation and economic growth" or "I want to examine the progress the Widget industry has made in improving productivity" or "We must ask ourselves what effect television is having on the minds of our youth."

Claims may be made implicit rather than explicit in some cases because the audience would be startled or even offended by a blunt statement of the speaker's case. There's nothing necessarily dishonest about the approach; it assumes that if the audience starts with an open mind the speaker will then have a chance to make a reasonable case for the claim. In many cases claims are implied because of what we might call social custom. The speaker starts off indirectly for the same reason a clerk in a store asks "May I help you?" rather than "May I sell you something?"

At any rate, the writer must identify the implied claim. Usually it will be obvious. When it is not, and this may be the case rather often with the subordinate claims to be examined later, the claim should actually be written out. This may be done conveniently by penciling the claim in the manuscript in brackets so the stated claim and the implied claim both appear on the page. The information in brackets would, of course, be only an aid for the speech writer and would not appear in the final manuscript.

A 1979 speech that had as its thesis "to assess business conditions" demonstrates an interesting case in which the speaker supplied his audience with implied claims and immediately made the claims explicit. Speaking at Southern Methodist University's School of Business, John McGillicuddy, Chairman of Manufacturers Hanover, previewed his main points this way:

> First, the immediate economic outlook, *which I do not see as nearly so bleak as sometimes portrayed.* Second, the impact on economic growth of the latest OPEC increases—*painful for many countries, including our own, but fully manageable.* Third, some observations on the President's energy proposals, *which I find encouraging in some respects, disappointing in others.* Finally, I will close [with] some personal observations. [*Vital Speeches,* September 15, 1979, p. 706. Emphasis supplied to set off the stated claims in the first three points.]

SUBORDINATE CLAIMS

When a writer uses the organizational scheme described in

Chapter IV, the thesis sentence will by definition establish the central claim made in the speech. That claim will be supported in the body of the speech by the main points which are subordinate claims. Yet another level of subordinate claims may be present if main points are further broken down into subpoints. The writer must identify the links in a chain of claims to make sure that a subordinate claim has a logical relationship to the broader claim under which it falls.

Taking as an example the speech, "Government Regulation: Slow Death for Free Enterprise," by Raymond C. Tower [*Vital Speeches*, September 1, 1980, pp. 676-80], this relationship may be readily traced. The thesis of the speech, the first main point, and the first set of subpoints are outlined below. In those instances in which the speaker implied the claim, an expressed claim has been supplied in brackets:

> *Thesis:* "I intend to talk to you today about the subject of excessive government regulation and particularly what I see as a possible outcome, the strangulation of our free enterprise system."
>
> *Main Point No. One:* "Let's look at the attack on the free enterprise system." [Excessive regulation is expensive, overwhelming, and ill motivated.]
>
> *Subpoint A:* "Business discussion on the regulatory assault often focuses on the costs we're forced to pay." [Regulation is expensive both directly and indirectly.]
>
> *Subpoint B:* "Our daily headlines read like the hospital chart of a very sick patient—all the vital signs are moving in the wrong direction. But what concerns me most is the range of foes pitted against the survival of the patient." [Regulators and their supporters are numerous.]
>
> *Subpoint C:* "The current regulatory assault is moralistic; it's self-righteous; it's emotional; it's naive."
>
>> *Sub-Subpoint 1:* "I say it's profoundly moralistic. . . ."
>>
>> *Sub-Subpoint 2:* "I say that the current onslaught is self-righteous. . . ."
>>
>> *Sub-Subpoint 3:* "I say that the current movement is highly emotional. . . ."
>>
>> *Sub-Subpoint 4:* "I say it's naive. . . ."

These, then, are the claims in the first point of a particular speech. Some of the claims are explicit ("I say it's naive") and some are implied ("Let's look at the nature of the attack"). With the claims located, the next matter of concern is an examination of the characteristics of claims. That examination will make it apparent why and how claims need to be supported.

Two Characteristics of Claims

Two sets of responses are possible when a claim is presented. First, a listener may understand or may not understand a claim. Of course, there are degrees of understanding. An audience willing to sit through a speech on Widget productivity probably has some notion of what the speaker means in claiming it must be improved. But if the audience's understanding is not up to the standard desired by the speaker, then the claim is "not understood."

Second, a claim may be believed or not believed. The speaker's hope is to have the audience at the same level of belief as the speaker by the end of the talk. If the aim of the speech is to inform, audience belief should not be an issue. If the aim of the speech is to stimulate, it is assumed that the audience already holds the belief and merely needs to be "stirred up."

The writer undertakes the task of making claims understandable and believable by supplying supporting material or evidence. This support *must directly follow any claim that appears at the end of a chain of claims.* The thesis statement of a speech, then, does not need immediate supporting evidence. The thesis is supported by the main points—the subordinate claims. (As it happens, the Tower speech *does* have material intervening between the thesis and the main point. This material, omitted from the above outline, supports the importance of the theme. This type of argument is usually not useful.)

In the Tower speech, Main Point No. One is built on subpoints, so it is not at the end of a chain and does not need support. Subpoints A and B are not further subdivided and must be supported. Subpoint C does not need direct evidence to support it, but the four claims into which it is divided must be backed up with evidence.

Types of Supporting Material

Writers have available five primary types of supporting

material. Based on the circumstances in which the speech is given, the writer can determine the combination of types of support needed to make claims believable and clear to the audience.

THE EXAMPLE

A specific instance can offer convincing proof of a claim. A specific instance, or example, is nothing more than one concrete case presented briefly. An example can be especially good in supporting a claim which attacks a broad generalization.

Claim: It's not true that you have to be a lawyer to get ahead in politics.

Examples: Look at Reagan and Carter.

Raymond Tower made excellent use of examples in backing up several of his claims. When he asserted that regulators and their supporters are numerous ("a range of forces"), he quickly cited four groups and three names of individuals: "the consumerists and environmentalists, the Friends of the Earth and the Foes of Nuclear Energy" and "the Ralph Naders, Mark Greens, and Jane Fondas."

THE ILLUSTRATION

The parables of the Bible and the stories of Abraham Lincoln offer strong proof of the value of telling a story to make a point. Lincoln's tales were often comic and the parables were always serious, but the effect in either case was to make an idea clear. Many times an illustration will not stand up under close scrutiny as logical evidence for a claim, but if other support is available for that purpose, the illustration serves a writer well in helping listeners understand.

In his Inaugural Address of January 20, 1981, President Ronald Reagan advanced the claim that the United States is a nation of heroes "with every right to dream heroic dreams." He specifically called attention to military heroes buried beneath "simple white markers" at nearby Arlington National Cemetery, and he cited examples of battlefields to drive home his point. Then he turned to an illustration for further support:

Under such a marker lies a young man, Martin Treptow, who left his job in a small town barber shop in 1917 to go to France with the famed Rainbow Division. There, on the Western front, he was killed trying to carry a message between battalions under heavy artillery fire. We are told that on his body was found a diary. On the flyleaf under the heading, "My Pledge," he had written these words: "America must win this war. Therefore I will work, I will save, I will sacrifice, I will endure, I will fight cheerfully and do my utmost, as if the issue of the whole struggle depended on me alone."

Returning to the Tower speech outlined above, one of the claims was that the attack on the free enterprise system is wrongly motivated. To support that claim, a subordinate claim was made that the attack grows out of emotion rather than facts. Here is how Tower backed up the last claim in his chain of arguments by supplying an illustration:

I say that the current movement is highly emotional and often without factual basis [CLAIM]. I imagine many of you saw the recent *National Geographic* article on "The Pesticide Dilemma," a depressing example of the emotionalism I'm talking about. It opened, you will recall, with a moving story about an itinerant worker believed to be dying from exposure to pesticide-related carcinogens. It went on to chronicle abuses in pesticide use and alleged harmful effects, without mentioning the enormous beneficial advances made in controlling pests, improving yields and increasing needed food supplies. The story closed on an unrelated and sensationalist note, speculating that the dying worker's daughter would one day be sorry she now romped in the sun through the fields when she, too, succumbed to her father's fatal affliction. And this, from one of the more distinguished journals in our country!

This illustration could, of course, have been shortened to an example just as any of the examples cited could have been expanded into illustrations.

THE ANALOGY

An excellent way to make a claim clear is to make it analogous with something the audience already knows. Analogy is sometimes called "the poorest form of argument," because to make a logical case the two things being compared must be alike in all respects except for the unknown feature the speaker needs to explain. Analogies seldom pass such a strict test of logic, but their power to explain remains unimpaired.

Tower used two analogies in quick succession. As he ended his claim that excessive regulation was costly, he said "It doesn't take an economic expert to understand that the U.S. economy is under severe strain. Our daily headlines read like the hospital chart of a very sick patient—all the vital signs are moving in the wrong direction." This analogy stresses the magnitude in the "cost claim," and it serves as a transition to the next claim, that the "range of forces" involved in regulation are numerous. Perhaps recognizing that an analogy is more for clarity than for believability, Tower said, "I don't want to exaggerate, but it's like sensing the distant hoofbeats of the Four Horsemen of the Apocalypse."

STATISTICS

In spite of the negative attitude some people have toward statistics, numbers can be useful in proving a point. Statistics can be made interesting as well as logical and should be used with a positive tone. Writers who start with the apologetic "I don't want to bore you with statistics, but. . . ." will put any speaker at a disadvantage.

Statistics will be more meaningful if they are rounded off and put in context. Almost no one in an audience will absorb the figure "$4,879,362.27," but "nearly five million dollars" might stick. Writing "4.7%" (which the speaker will read as the deadly dull "four-point-seven percent) is not as good as "about five percent" which is not as good as "about one out of twenty." Naturally there will be times when the precise figure is called for.

Here is a case where a speaker took some mind-numbing numbers and made sense of them. Mr. Barrie L. Jones, Vice President of Howard Chase, made the claim that public relations professionals need to "understand scale" to do their jobs well. He supported that claim with statistics:

> Let me give you an example of scale in our own turf. I collected press releases reporting third quarter earnings from ten of the major oil companies. These announcements were made during the week of October 22-31. Let's take the Phillips 66 press release to illustrate the value of scale. Now, why don't you take out a pencil and a

piece of paper. I need your help with some math. Please write down
these figures. In its third quarter, Phillips 66 reported revenues of
$2,500,000,000. In round numbers, its earnings for the quarter were
$190,000,000. Now, take your pencil and eliminate the last three
digits in both revenues and earnings. That gives us revenues of
$2,500,000 and earnings of $190,000. Got your pencils ready? O.K.,
let's cross out the last three digits again. Now, Phillips' revenues are
$2,500 and its earnings are $190. Isn't this fun? Let's do it again.
But this time just knock out one digit from both revenues and earnings. Now we have revenues of $250 and earnings of $19. My experience in financial matters is no where near the level of competence represented in this room. But can anyone of you tell me that
the severest critics will find earnings of $19 on revenues of $250 an
unacceptably high return? [*Vital Speeches,* January 15, 1980, p. 217]

Again we find the Tower speech demonstrating the relationship between claim and evidence. Statistics are used to support
the "cost" claim. Several figures are cited, but in one passage
Tower builds the data to an interesting climax: ". . . the regulatory costs incurred in just one year for the sample companies
amounted to 10 percent of their aggregate capital expenditures,
16 percent of their after-tax profits, and fully 46 percent of
their research and development expenditures. That's a significant
burden!"

A speech writer's sense of logic, along with the critical read-
ings a speech gets in the approval process, should be enough to
make sure statistics are fair and accurate. The writer's biggest
job is to make them clear and interesting.

QUOTES

A quote can help make a claim understandable and believable in two ways. First, because it may state the idea well. Some
speakers who would not dare be caught in public with an
eloquent phrase of their own, will allow a well-worded idea to
appear if it is a quotation from someone else. Second, a quote
can bring to bear the testimony of an expert to supplement the
authority of the speaker.

Often a quote can combine these two virtues. John Hanley
used such a quotation in support of a claim that the controlled
use of chemicals should be allowed in food production:

The respected nutritionist, Dr. Jean Mayer, has said that the public must try to "distinguish between real problems, unsupported claims, and the mouthings of food cranks. Otherwise," Dr. Mayer says, "there may soon be a national tendency to eat nothing but bean sprouts and alfalfa, on which a few deluded souls have already undertaken to survive."

Raymond Tower also uses both features of the quotation when he supports his claim that supporters of excessive regulation are "naive" by citing economist Herbert Stein's description of them as members of the "Woodstock School" of economics.

In using quotations, a speech writer should not become a quotehanger who scatters quotes through a speech with wild abandon. While there can be no firm rule, three or four quotes in a fifteen to twenty minute speech do not seem excessive. Using ten or more almost certainly has crossed the boundary.

Quotes should be kept short. Paraphrase all but the "good parts" or, as Hanley does, break the quote up. A long quote will challenge the delivery skills of the best speakers, and the worst ones will put their audiences to sleep.

Avoid writing the words "quote" and "end quote." They sound strange. If the speaker's voice does not signal the end of the quote, tell the audience the quote is over by writing a tag line such as "I believe Mr. Expert's words offer sound advice" or write in a transition to the next idea. Most of the time a pause or a change in tone will be enough.

No writer should ever stoop to inventing quotations, but in fact should take great pains to make sure of the accuracy of a quote before using it. A writer should also be realistic about what a speaker can reasonably expect to have read. Quotes culled from collections can make a speaker look foolish. In one case a person doing research for a speech took Brutus' line "There is a tide in the affairs of men. . . ." from a book of quotations and in his notes recorded only the play as the source. Having no knowledge at all of Shakespeare, the speaker then stood before a college audience and read, "As Julius Caesar once said. . . ."

ADDITIONAL FORMS OF SUPPORT

Although examples, illustration, analogy, statistics, and quotations are the primary means of supporting a claim, a few additional types are worth noting. Explanation can be used to support a point. The speaker says, "What I mean is. . . ." to fix a claim in the listener's mind without actually bringing any evidence to bear on the point. Restatement and repetition may be used. Martin Luther King Jr.'s "I have a dream" statement made his point stronger with each repetition. Descriptions, definitions, and even mild expletives ("Now, how about that!") could help build a claim.

The five types of support discussed in detail above remain the basic evidence on which a claim will stand or fall. As an interesting experiment, a writer might go through the body of a speech manuscript carefully drawing lines through the five kinds of evidence. The object of the experiment would be to see how much was left unmarked. In theory at least, the only unmarked lines would be the claims plus any language used for such purposes as summary or transition. If a great deal is left unmarked, the manuscript is probably a mass of claims supported by other claims with no solid evidence to help an audience understand or believe.

TYPES OF PROOF

Early in the history of the study of public speaking the classical rhetoricians asked a question of fundamental importance. What causes a listener to accept a speaker's ideas? Gradually, the theory emerged that all the kinds of evidence speakers use could be classified in one or more of three categories of proof. The three kinds of proof were accepted as the forces that caused listeners to believe or act.

The categories of proof are (1) the logic of the argument, (2) the emotions felt by the audience, and (3) the person of the speaker. A given piece of evidence in a speech, then, can build a logical case for the claim, create an emotional response favorable to the claim, or bring out qualities of the speaker that might influence the listener to accept the claim.

While the classical division of proof may not be a fully adequate explanation of human behavior (to a behaviorist of the B. F. Skinner school, for example), it provides a roughly accurate guide to the forces that guide many of our daily activities.

Are we influenced, sometimes, by logic? The answer is yes for anyone in the market for a lawn mower who first went to a consumer magazine to gather facts on the quality of various brands. (Of course, emotional motivation in the form of greed is not entirely absent.)

Are we influenced, sometimes, by emotion? The answer is yes for any homeowner who has replaced a battered and ugly but serviceable lawn mower to avoid the shame of being outclassed by the shiney new mower next door.

Are we influenced, sometimes, by the person of a persuader? Yes, if anyone buys a lawn mower from a friend who owns a hardware store instead of buying a cheaper or higher quality model from a stranger.

At a practical level, then, the categories are useful. A speech writer should make sure that a speech contains evidence from all three categories.

LOGICAL PROOF

To simplify a rather complicated subject, logical proof can be said to consist of supplying enough examples, illustrations, analogies, statistics, and/or quotations to satisfy the audience that the claim advanced is reasonable. The process involves both quality and quantity.

The quality of the evidence depends on its accuracy and its relevance to the claim being made. Once the accuracy of data is verified, a writer can establish relevance only if the claim has been clearly isolated. To be logical, the evidence must intelligently reinforce the claim. If a speaker makes the claim "It was wrong to forbid prayer in public schools," and supports the claim by citing the rise in the number of students enrolling in private schools, there is little doubt of the accuracy of the evidence. But the evidence clearly fails the test of relevance. It doesn't support the claim.

The quantity of evidence needed may be harder to determine. How much is enough? A single example may prove a point in some cases. In another instance a dozen pieces of evidence drawn from all five of the types may barely do the job. The writer must decide.

EMOTION

Recognizing that listeners are moved by their emotions does not mean that the speech or the speaker will be emotional. Rather, it means that emotions of the audience must be taken into account in choosing material to back up claims.

Appeals to the emotions are common in everyday communication. We find them in advertising and in normal conversational exchanges at home or at work. A speech on almost any controversial topic will be delivered to an audience that has already had its emotions appealed to by persuaders on the other side of the argument.

In any society most people are motivated by the same basic emotional drives. The list below includes some but not all the emotions which impel a typical modern Western audience:

Fear. Greed. Love. Friendship. Independence. Conformity. Fair Play. Patriotism. Sympathy. Security. Recognition.

President Reagan's Martin Treptow illustration appealed strongly to patriotism and sympathy. Barrie L. Jones's statistics on Phillips 66 return compared to revenue appealed to fair play. Raymond Tower appealed to greed in telling business executives of the cost of regulation (although other appeals were also present), and he appealed to fear in warning of the huge number of regulators and their supporters. Even when attacking the emotionalism of supporters of regulation with his illustration of the story from *National Geographic,* Tower himself used emotion in appealing to fair play.

No speech writer is likely to go out with a shopping list of emotional appeals and systematically gather a bagful to put in a speech. In the normal course of writing a speech, they will usually appear. Knowledge of the specifics of motive appeals helps the speech writer primarily in the editing process.

It is often useful to read a manuscript through for a single purpose. This might be done to check the use of emotional appeals (just as one reading might be limited to checking organization or another to checking the vividness of language).

In editing for emotional appeals, a writer should first make sure the speech has not been made purely logical with no concern for audience feeling. Then the variety of appeals should be studied. A writer may easily slip into the habit of relying excessively on one or two appeals—fear and greed, for example. Part of the concern in checking for variety is to make sure some of the nobler appeals get included. Finally, motives should not be dictated. President Reagan did not say "If we have any patriotism in our hearts, we must respect the sacrifice of Martin Treptow." The President simply told the story.

PERSON OF THE SPEAKER

A writer would be making a serious error to neglect the use of the speaker's character as a means of persuasion. When it is neglected, the reason seems to be the fear speakers and writers have that references to the speaker will appear egotistical. Add to that the drill many writers have had in avoiding the personal pronoun, and the obstacles to using the speaker's character may be formidable.

But speaking is a personal means of communication. And ego is less a function of what is said than it is of that mysterious force we call personality. People who are egotistical reveal their ego in manner more than in ideas. They show their ego in style and tone. A modest person can speak of great accomplishments modestly, but an egotistical person speaks egotistically of the weather.

The speaker's character can appear in a speech by showing the speaker's knowledge, concern, and integrity. These useful aspects of personal proof may be referred to as "I know," "I care," and "I am not a crook." All the examples cited are taken from a single issue of *Vital Speeches* [February 1, 1980].

I Know. Indicating a speaker's personal knowledge of the subject of a speech involves two steps. First, examples, illustrations, statistics, analogies, and quotations should be based where possible on the speaker's experience. Second, the speaker's first-hand acquaintance with the material should be made clear to the audience. "I saw," "I read," "I recall," and "I went" are all simple phrases that can turn a routine piece of evidence into impressive support for a claim. "The latest figures reveal" can often be replaced with "I studied with care the facts we recently collected. . . ."

Here is how Postmaster General William Bolger gave a dramatic touch to an otherwise routine quotation in support of his claim that public attitude affects inflation. "To quote a young woman I heard interviewed recently, 'Why should I care if the price of a "Big Mac" goes from $1.69 to $1.99 or whatever, as long as my wages go up, too.' " [p. 241]

To illustrate his point that supervision is important, Timken Company President Joseph Toot said, "To put this thesis in sharp focus for all of us, permit me to use as a vehicle an incident that occurred at one of my company's bearing manufacturing plants several months ago. This example may not be an especially dramatic one, but I would submit that it illustrates quite well the kinds of things than can fall apart when there is a failure of supervision. An operator in the plant to which I refer was responsible for running two screw machines. . . . [p. 237. In order to call attention to the fact that illustrations hold interest through curiosity, as was pointed out in the previous chapter, this story will be left unfinished.]

I Care. Statements of concern are powerful when sincere. They appear in daily conversation, and they can be easily added to speeches. In almost any speech manuscript written in an impersonal style, three or four paragraphs can usually be found where it would be quite natural to add an additional line. Assuming that the statement would be true, it would simply say "And I want you to know I am deeply concerned about this matter" or "We at Ajax are determined to keep our service at this high level."

Here are some examples of expressed concern from the same issue of *Vital Speeches* mentioned above:

> I know that what I'm saying isn't the popular thing to say. But I am convinced it must be done. [Postmaster General Bolger, p. 242]
> Let me make it clear, I do not question the good intentions of all the vast army of men and women who operate the agencies and bureaus that spend billions of our tax dollars. [Hearst Foundation Executive Director Charles Gould, p. 235]
> I'm not saying that everything will be business as usual. It won't. But I don't find that bad,—I find it invigorating. [Allan W. Ostar,

President of the American Association of State Colleges and Universities, p. 243]

But I do not despair. I think there will be tremendous opportunities in the '80s and '90s. I believe we can and will overcome many of our current problems. [Robert J. Buckley, Chairman and President of Allegheny Ludlum, p. 251]

I Am Not A Crook. Demonstrating a speaker's integrity presents a writer with a delicate problem. Queen Gertrude's terse "The lady doth protest too much" reminds us of the dangers of a too ostentatious show of honor. But occasions arise when a direct statement of the speaker's honesty should be made.

Postmaster General Bolger establishes his candor indirectly in his defense of the efficiency of the mails: "Individual lapses will, and do, occur; they always have. But I think any fairminded person would allow this is inevitable when we are dealing with 300 millions items." [p. 241]

And John Caldwell, International Vice President of the Chamber of Commerce, hastens to spell out his moral stand after making an attack on what he considered to be a selective application of a human rights policy: "It is also interesting to note that human rights violations committed by Israel seem to enjoy far less publicity in our press than petty features of South Africa's policy of apartheid—which, incidentally, I do not condone either." [p. 252]

THE COMPLEXITY OF EVIDENCE AND PROOF

At no point in this discussion is it implied that the types of evidence and the categories of proof are neatly compartmentalized in the actual presentation of a speech. An illustration may include statistics and a quotation may contain an analogy. A logical example may appeal to fear, and a statement of concern may evoke a strong feeling of patriotism in an audience. Listeners are not targets in a shooting gallery with so many points awarded for a logical statistic and so many points for an emotional example.

But the ability to identify elements of proof and types of evidence gives a writer a system for evaluating a speech. An appreciation of the classical approach to proof, like an understanding of good organization, can and should be creative.

Comprehending the relationship between claims and support ought to broaden a writer's options while at the same time helping produce sound speeches.

A NOTE ON HANDLING COUNTER ARGUMENTS

At times a writer knows an audience will be aware of arguments against the position being taken in a speech. Or perhaps the counter arguments soon will be made public. In such a case it is better to get the counter arguments out into the open.

Research conducted over the past thirty years suggests intelligent and well informed audiences will be more easily convinced if they hear both sides in a controversy. They are also more likely to stay convinced longer if they hear both points of view while making up their minds.

These results square with common sense. A speaker confident and candid enough to bring out opposing arguments exerts a strong appeal, and the counter arguments an audiences hears afterwards from another source will have lost some of their power to dissuade because they have already been taken into account.

STRATEGIES

A writer can choose from among three basic strategies. The counter argument can be granted, balanced, or refuted.

Grant the Counter Argument. Few corporate executives or government officials like to come right out and say good arguments can be made against positions they take. But such a course may be sound. Owen Butler, Chairman of the Board of Procter and Gamble, thought so in defending Procter and Gamble's sponsorship of TV programs under attack for excessive sex and violence. [*Vital Speeches*, August 1, 1981] Butler made the claim in his speech that Proctor and Gamble remained "perfectly willing to defend" the show, *White Shadow*, in spite of certain controversial episodes. Then he conceded a point to his critics. "What we can't defend is the pre-show publicity which included ads placed without our knowledge and featuring the headline 'Teacher Seduces Student.'" Although Butler's immediate audience was made up of professional TV people, his granting of an argument that had been published in a Federation of Decency newsletter was no doubt aimed in part at a distant audience.

Another example may be seen in a speech delivered by a U.S. military officer at a historically black university. The address developed a theme of black progress in the armed services. The audience responded well, and the speech won support for the military. The text of the address, however, offered many instances of the *failure* of the military to do a better job of giving equal treatment, and the speech ignored many recent improvements. This approach might seem backward at first, but it bears out research findings suggesting at times granting the correctness of opposition arguments may be the best way to handle them. Had the military speaker devoted his time to a rosy account of progress, many listeners would have blocked out his message while thinking about the counter arguments.

Granting a counter argument does not mean the speaker has to grovel. In fact, it is usually a good idea to avoid words such as "concede" and "admit." The speaker can "recognize" or "realize" or "be aware of" counter arguments without appearing weak.

Balancing Counter Arguments. A writer may deal with opposition points by bringing them up and balancing them off with points on the speaker's side of the issue. This method still involves granting the negative point, but it doesn't stop there. An example of how the method should *not* be used appears in Postmaster Bolger's statement cited above that in handling the mail "individual lapses do occur" but the postal service deals with "the daily movement of 300 million items." This is a "yes, but not quite" type of argument that gives with one hand and takes away with the other. A writer may choose to develop a point in this way, but it should be recognized that the Bolger example represents a mild attempt at the third method of handling counter arguments—refutation. A true balancing argument says "Yes, Bluto's Ice Cream is the most expensive in the world." Then the argument adds, "And we will keep it expensive so that you can continue to have cream imported from Devonshire and vanilla beans hand-picked by the light of the full-moon."

Refuting Counter Arguments. The third approach to counter arguments, and perhaps the most common except for ignoring them, calls for the writer to show they are wrong. In the aftermath of the Love Canal controversy, the president of Hooker Chemical, Donald L. Baeder, took on the arguments against his company and his industry. His defense was bold. Apparent concessions to opposition arguments turn out not to be concessions after all: "First, we *do* have a problem . . . but it is not the problem that is commonly perceived" and "Candidly, we in the chemical industry must share part of the blame for public skepticism . . . because we generally did not do enough to explain our efforts to the public." [*Vital Speeches,* June 1, 1980, pp. 496-500]

Baeder attacked charges of past industry irresponsibility head-on. Using analogies with changes that have occurred in scientific understanding of dealing with x-rays and asbestos, he built a case that the chemical industry should not be judged "using today's standards applied to *past* practices or for not knowing what was *unknowable* at the time."

CONCLUSION

Long ago Aristotle concluded that the essense of the art of speaking was to discover in each individual case all the means of persuasion available to the speaker. At the heart of that process is the determination of the claims to be made and the material at hand to support those claims. Identifying claims and supporting them adequately can be a difficult and even a tedious business. But it is a necessary business for the writer who wants a speech to be more than a string of glittering generalities.

CHAPTER VI

LANGUAGE

"I am by calling a dealer in words, and words are, of course, the most powerful drug used by mankind."
[Rudyard Kipling in a speech before the Royal College of Surgeons]

Words do make a difference. Those who claim the idea is everything—and such people seem to come rather often from the ranks of the scientific and technically minded—are wrong. Words without ideas will never amount to much, but ideas need to be articulated well to have an impact.

The writer works with but two variables—word choice and word combination. The whole matter of style boils down finally to choosing one word over another and then selecting the best possible combination of words.

When an American general said "Nuts" in answer to a Nazi surrender demand in World War II, he chose the right word to make his message last. When John F. Kennedy strung together the words "ask, not, what, your, country, can, do, for, you," he selected ordinary words but cast them in an order that made his phrase one of the most quoted passages in modern public speaking. Churchill demonstrated the mastery of both word choice and word combination in such phrases as "blood, tears, toil, and sweat."

Can the manipulation of the variables be learned by someone wishing to improve? Teaching style always works better after the fact. That is to say, anyone who wishes to teach the effective use of language can do a far better job of singling out good examples than straightening out bad habits. Columnist James J. Kilpatrick takes a pessimistic view in his statement "none of us can explain what is meant by style and none of us can tell someone else how to go about acquiring style." [Kilpatrick, *Richmond News-Leader,* September 12, 1981]

Although it is far easier to learn new patterns of organization or fresh ways to use evidence than it is to change language habits, two areas of study can help writers produce better speeches. The first of these areas is the study of the distinctive features of "oral" language as opposed to language to be read silently, and the second is a review of selected basics that apply to all good writing but have a particular value in writing speeches.

ORAL LANGUAGE

We don't use the same language to express an idea in speaking that we use in writing. As a well-known professor of public speaking once put it, "A speech is not an essay standing on its hind legs." A great British orator, Charles James Fox, insisted that a speech that read well in the newspaper was sure to have been a bad speech. And lawyer Louis Nizer noted that "even great writers and poets who are experts in molding words are often helpless in the realm of speaking. Public speaking must be recognized as a separate art. . . . The words may be the same, but the grammar, rhetoric and phrasing are different. It is a different mode of expression—a different language." [Nizer, p. 22]

Our educational system allows few opportunities to put "speaking language" down on paper. Much formal training in writing actually discourages any effort to capture the language of speech on the printed page. Speech writers with an established record of successful business, journalistic, or academic writing may find they have to break old habits.

One quite simple device will catch most of the words and phrases in a speech that strike the ear as wrong. The writer should read the speech into a tape recorder. Some changes can be made on the basis of how the words "feel" as they are read. When the tape is played back, a few more awkward spots can be fixed.

By reading and hearing the speech in draft form and by remembering a few of the characteristics of oral language described below, a writer should be able to produce a manuscript that captures the flavor of speech. It is important to remember that only the "flavor" of conversational speech is desired. Good language for a manuscript speech is *not* exactly the same as that of normal conversation. Cleaned up and taken out of the manuscript will be vocalizations such as "and, ah" or "er." Also missing for the most part will be a number of what we might call non-words sprinkled through much conversation in the form of "mmmmmm," "huh?," and "hah." Much of the twisted syntax present when a speaker gropes for a thought will obviously be missing too.

WORDINESS

Writers have generally been taught to regard conciseness as a virtue in style. The injunction to write concisely has its roots in the principle that no more words should be used than are necessary to communicate a thought. That principle holds for speech as well as writing, but its application is different. In part because of the instantaneous nature of communication in speaking, most ideas require more words to be understood in speaking than would be needed in silent reading. The object remains the same in speech as in reading—to use no more than the number of words needed to communicate successfully.

Speakers add words in an effort to get their ideas across in three ways. They repeat ideas, they stretch out ideas, and they pile on more evidence than they would use in most writing.

Repetition. Writers for the eye as well as writers for the ear may on at least a few occasions find it useful to repeat. In the Declaration of Independence, Thomas Jefferson, by no means an orator, leveled seventeen consecutive charges against King George all beginning with the phrase "he has." He wrote seven clauses in a row starting with the word "for," and in the span of four sentences he included four "we have's" and one "nor have we."

The Declaration, however, was a distinctly oratorical piece of writing, and repetition is not as common in print as it is in such passages as "I have a dream" from Martin Luther King Jr. or Churchill's "We shall fight on the beaches. We shall fight on the landing grounds. We shall fight in the fields and in the streets, and we shall fight in the hills."

Repetition does not always call for reusing words. Ideas may be restated in fresh language. For example, Marilyn Loden, District Staff Manager for New York Telephone, in a speech on "networking" for women, drove an idea home by stating it four times: "When you develop or join a network, others outside the system view it as a threat. You run the risk of being perceived as an agitator, a troublemaker. There is always something unsettling when people get together with a sense of seriousness and purpose. In the case of a women's network, there will always be some men and women who view such a group with suspicion." [*Vital Speeches*, August 1, 1981, p. 615]

Stretching Out. "Nuts" was a rhetorically satisfactory answer for General McAuliffe to give the Nazis, but when using an oral style a sentence may be stretched out even to the point of redundancy. For example, a sign saying "Tow-Away Zone" presents all the basic information a driver needs to learn a particular piece of information. But the owner of a cafe in a small Texas town produced a much more "conversational" version: "No Parking. Violators Will Be Towed Away At Owner's Expense." The word "away" is clearly redundant (where else would they be towed but "away"?), and the claim that "violators" will be towed (rather than vehicles) is inaccurate. We might assume that the author of the sign would fare better as a speech writer than as a newspaper editor.

In a speech discussing a series of periods of history, an early draft contained the phrase "from 1946 to 1969." To help the audience absorb the idea—and to help separate more emphatically this period of time from others in the speech, the phrase was stretched in a later draft. It then read, "during the more than twenty years from the end of World War II to the close of the 1960s." The second version has three times as many words as the first, it gives the number of years as well as the time span contained in the first draft, and it uses extra words to give landmarks at the beginning and the end of period in question.

Adding Evidence. Obviously a writer may choose to support a claim in a report with as much evidence as would be used in a speech. But often the written claim will require far less support. A limited amount of evidence can be submitted on the assumption that the reader can absorb the full impact of whatever is presented. A listener, on the other hand, might be expected to need a greater quantity of evidence because it goes by so quickly. Marilyn Loden's networking speech indicates how speakers often "pile up" evidence to make a point: "Working women are deluged today with recipes for success. Walk into any bookstore and you'll find a dozen books loaded with advice for the working woman on "how to dress for success,' how to become more assertive, how to learn the corporate 'games mother never taught you,' how to prepare gourmet meals in 10 minutes. I could go on all night with these 'how to's.' " [*Vital Speeches*, August 1, 1981, p. 614]

Because an idea takes more words to develop in speaking than it does in writing, a speech writer might be well advised to make special efforts to limit the scope of a speech. A speaker may want to take on too broad a subject. Quite often a topic can be cut in half or even slashed to a third of its original scope. The remainder could then be made into a much better talk than would be possible with the broader subject.

INFORMAL WORD CHOICE

A speaker once referred to the laser as an invention that has the scientific world "agog." The audience was probably agog for a minute or two at hearing a word seldom spoken in informal speaking. In a speech to company employees, a high-ranking corporate officer began to discuss fringe benefits by saying "as you contemplate retirement. . . ." The efforts the company was making to show concern for its employees was no doubt dampened somewhat by the word "contemplate"—a perfectly decent word in print—that sounded stiff and formal in a speech that was supposed to be warm and caring.

The simple little word "for" has no place in a speech if used in the sense of "because." It *looks* fine, but it *sounds* out of place as anyone can tell by reading aloud the simple sentence, "I wanted to meet you, for I have heard a lot about you." Many words ending in -ly strike the ear as too formal: "firstly" for "first", "importantly" for "important," or "alternatively" for the phrase "as an alternative." Starting sentences with -ing words often sounds odd, as in the sentence "Being hungry, we stopped to eat."

Words that refer to physical locations in a manuscript, commonly used in writing, should be avoided in speeches. "Above" and "below" are good examples. Even "following" and "preceding" refer as much to space as to time and should rarely be used.

The list could be expanded. Usually "on" sounds better than "upon," "also" better than "moreover, " "find out" better than "ascertain," and "that" better than "which." Words with an archaic ring (whence, hence, thus, whereupon) are generally out of place. Of course, in quotations or in an deliberate effort to achieve formality, some of the formal language of writing can be effective. No suggestion about style can be firm without knowing the context in which the language appears.

Nothing has been said here about jargon. Jargon represents a problem not of formality but of clarity and will be discussed later. Understanding the speaker is not the point now being raised. All of the words criticized so far make perfectly good sense to a normal person. The employees *understood* 'contemplate," but the word destroyed the desired tone of the message.

Some authorities on speech claim speaking uses shorter words than writing. As the above examples demonstrate, that rule does not always apply. A speech writer needs "talking words" no matter how long they may be.

RHYTHM

While a speech should not have the firm cadence of "The Charge of the Light Brigade," rhythm is slightly more important in speech than in written prose. Occasionally a sentence in print jars a reader because the beat is off, but the harm is not as great as in the case of speaking.

One writer's sense of rhythm may not be the same as that of another writer. But the simplest way to judge cadence is to depend on the ear. The first sentence below has a flaw in its rhythm. Reading it aloud should suggest a change.

> He marched through corporate America leaving a trail behind him of profit and growth.

One solution to the problem is to invert two pairs of words to produce, "He marched through corporate America leaving behind him a trail of profit and growth." Now the sentence flows in the manner of normal speech.

Climax. At times a writer wants to punch up a thought by

making it the climax of a sentence or a paragraph. Rhythm, including the proper use of the pause, can create the climax. The sentence used as an illustration above could be changed to read, "He marched through corporate America leaving behind him a trail of profit—and of growth."

Climax often depends in part on the increasing importance of the ideas being expressed. A speech by Under Secretary of the Navy James Woolsey illustrates that approach in a passage that has excellent rhythm: "The least desirable way to achieve victory is to destroy an enemy's cities; the next least desirable is to kill his soldiers; better is to destroy his alliances; but best of all is to destroy his plans and never have to fight at all." [*Vital Speeches*, July 1, 1978] This sentence has climactic order with a conversational tone.

Clauses. Speech writers should avoid clauses. They should write sentences in a straightforward subject, verb, object order. Clauses ask a listener to hold in mind the idea in the first part of the sentence while a new or qualifying idea is injected. Readers can handle clauses; listeners have difficulty with them.

At times, clauses not only suspend an idea, they run the risk of insulting the audience. This will occur almost any time a clause is used to insert a person's qualifications. For example, if a speaker says "Will Rogers, the famous humorist from Oklahoma, once said. . . ." the audience is told, in effect, "Will Rogers, and since you don't know who he is, I'll tell you. . . ." The qualification could simply be dropped in some cases. When it can't, when a few members of the audience may *not* know who Will Rogers was or when it is important for some reason to make sure everyone remembers he was from Oklahoma, then the clause must be removed without eliminating the information. The sentence could properly read, "That famous Oklahoma humorist Will Rogers once said. . . ."

Clauses can also be removed when they qualify things. "I once lived in Alabama, a state deep in the heart of the American South, where. . . ." becomes "I once lived deep in the heart of the American South in the state of Alabama where. . . ." The revised phrase has a better rhythm. Also, by moving from the general to the specific case rather than the other way around, it avoids offending the listener.

When a writer finds it appropriate to insert material in the middle of a sentence, the insertion should be set off with dashes rather than with commas. If an idea is important enough to interrupt a sentence, it should be done with more emphasis than that suggested by the punctuation of an ordinary clause.

Here are a couple of examples of dashes in Professor Andrew Cecil's address, "Independence and World Citizenship." [*Vital Speeches,* August 1, 1980]

> The alternative—God save us—is to perish together.
> Crimes against humanity—the atrocities of arrest without trial, torture, and concentration camps—are not solved at these conferences.

Usually a speaker will make a more abrupt pause at a dash than a comma. Also, speakers are more likely to change vocal inflection to emphasize material set off by dashes.

THE SPOKEN SENTENCE

The sentence of impromptu conversation bears little resemblance to the sentence of formal, written English. As in other aspects of style, the sentence of a manuscript speech borrows from both the spoken and the written form.

A spoken sentence can be quite long. Short units of thought connected by "and" or "but" form a single grammatical string that can stretch for hundreds of words. When such a construction is used, it is meaningless to argue that "long sentences are harder to understand than short sentences." The argument may be correct for long *complex* sentences with many clauses, but spoken sentences are generally free of clauses. A more accurate statement would be "long thought units are harder to understand than short thought units." A page in this book could easily be filled with a sentence a speaker could convey with little difficulty.

On paper, even in a speech manuscript, such a sentence would look strange. But speech writers capture the essence of the long sentence flow by putting periods before the conjunctions and starting many new sentences with "and" or "but." If the sentences express worthwhile ideas, writers should not be deterred from starting them with conjunctions simply because of the rules in some style book.

Speech writers should be more concerned with variety of length than with keeping sentences short. A few one-word or two-word sentences can liven up a talk. If all the sentences are kept at about the same length, the speech will probably sound monotonous.

Fragments. Speech writers may add variety to a talk by including an occasional sentence fragment. Ronald Reagan's Inaugural Address had several incomplete sentences in it. Here are two in just one paragraph:

> Professionals, industrialists, shopkeepers, clerks, cabbies and truck drivers. They are, in short, "We the people." This breed called Americans.

The sentence fragment in a manuscript looks somewhat more like a deliberate rhetorical device than a reflection of normal speech patterns. That appears to be true in the Reagan example. But fragments abound in normal speech. "No way." "Lots of luck." "A hundred dollars!" "Wonderful, wonderful, wonderful."

Rhetorical Questions. Like the sentence fragment, the rhetorical question adds variety to the language of a speech. It has two additional virtues. It helps bridge the gap between the speaker and the audience. A question attempts to break through to the audience, to engage the listener's mind. Also, the rhetorical question adds a dramatic note. An issue is phrased in a compelling way; questions imply mystery and perhaps even a sense of urgency. A question can forcefully draw attention to a speaker's point: "What can we do, then, to restore the vitality of American industry? I say we must redouble our efforts in research and development."

The dramatic effect of a rhetorical question may be enhanced by presenting it as coming from someone else. "Our critics ask" or "the responsible buyer must wonder how we are able. . . ."

Rhetorical questions have an even greater impact when several are used together. In arguing that corporations should give five percent of their profits to charity, Kenneth N. Dayton groups three questions. Phrasing his questions as though they came from the audience, he said, "At this point you might ask, 'Why five percent?' Why strive for the maximum? Why not go along with the national average of about one percent?' " At another point Dayton clusters three questions to stress the benefits of corporate contributions: "How many Lyric Theatres would that build? How much cancer research would that fund? How many Hispanic programs?" [*Vital Speeches,* August 1, 1980, pp. 619-622]

While rhetorical questions are usually phrased to elicit an answer in the affirmative, at times they may be designed to stress the negative. On the theory that an audience may be stronger in its opposition to what it *dislikes* than in support for what it *likes,* writers may find this approach useful. Patrick Henry fired a barrage of negative questions in one of the most famous speeches in American history. In an effort to persuade his audience to vote to prepare for war in his famous "Give Me Liberty or Give Me Death" speech, he said, "They tell us, Sir, that we are weak; unable to cope with so formidable an adversary. But when shall we be stronger? Will it be next week or next year? Will it be when we are totally disarmed, and when a British guard shall be stationed in every house? Shall we gather strength by irresolution and inaction?"

Rhetorical questions must be used with some caution. Except in most unusual cases they must be truly rhetorical and neither demand nor permit a verbal response from an audience. Audiences are quite reluctant to give an overt, honest answer to a speaker. Listeners tend to be passive, and if the speaker asks, "Let me see the hands of those who support safe driving," the response may be far from accurate. And it may cause the speaker to look foolish if the next sentence in the speech is based on a response that did not materialize. Just as bad is the question that does get an audible response when none is desired. If a writer expects listeners to be boisterous or unfriendly or drunk, rhetorical questions may not be wise.

PERSONAL WORDS

In the fine guide to style by William Strunk as revised by E. B. White, the first of the positive suggestions for improving writing calls for the writer to be kept in the background. The "mood and temper" of the writer should not be obvious in the language of good writing. However valuable this rule may be for the writer of reports and essays, it does not apply to the writer for spoken discourse. The personality of the speaker *should* emerge, and personal language will appear frequently in good speeches.

The use of "personal proof," discussed earlier, demands personal language in a speech. So does the social nature of the speaking situation; speakers who never use the personal pronoun will appear too formal and distant for most public presentations. The speech writer faces the problem not of weeding out personal references but rather of finding ways to get them into a speech. The writer must know what the speaker can say with personal conviction and convince the speaker that such material should be in the manuscript.

Major General Rufus Billups, in a speech at a Black Heritage Week Banquet, set the tone for his address with the following statement: "As I look at the situation in America, today, I could make an assumption that many Black Americans would be surprised and elated to learn of the remarkable achievements by Blacks throughout the history of America, and of the world. I, too, have been enlightened over the years, and consequently, I want very much to share some of that knowledge of our Black people with you at this most appropriate time." [*Vital Speeches,* September 15, 1979, p. 712] General Billups's language makes his speech a personal statement rather than merely a recitation of historical events.

CHARACTERISTICS OF ALL GOOD LANGUAGE

Three characteristics of all good writing should guide speech writers in choosing and arranging words. The language of a speech should be clear, vivid, and appropriate.

CLARITY

Making ideas clear starts with understanding how meaning is transferred in communication. Unfortunately, much schooling and practice in writing focuses on the "correctness" of language rather than on how words carry meaning. As a result, writers concentrate on the rules of grammar or the meaning in a dictionary. A better starting point for the speech writer would be a study of semantics—the study of "how words mean."

Semantics explores the relationship between words and the concepts words convey. At the heart of this relationship is the realization that a word is but a symbol for an object or a concept in the speaker's mind. As the semanticists put it, "The word is not the thing."

The use of technical language illustrates the point. Technical experts are sometimes so concerned about the "right" word they forget that the word is but a symbol for the idea. Take the word "station," for example, as it is used by engineers in the telephone industry. It means almost the same thing as "telephone." Because there is a subtle difference between the two terms, many engineers resist the advice to use the almost correct term, telephone. The result is that most lay listeners are mystified by references to large numbers of "stations" in an engineer's speech. Like many technical terms, "station" is so difficult to explain, the required explanation would seldom be worth the trouble. The almost correct term would do a far better job of making the engineer's idea *clear* to an audience.

Precise technical language obviously has its role when one expert talks to another. Saying "telephone" instead of "station" could conceivably be a confusing and even costly mistake when one engineer communicates with another. The writer's concern, then, must be on how the symbol gets interpreted rather than on the so-called "true meaning" of a term.

The relationship of words and their referents may be seen in the diagram below. Note that only the listener links the symbol and the concept.

The semantics approach to language suggests that meaning is found in people rather than in words. If the writer chooses a symbol that the listener associates with the concept in the speech, then the language is clear. Clarity is not achieved simply because the writer and the speaker understand the words.

Even when a listener understands the words in a speech, the language will not clearly transmit the ideas of the speaker if the words distract. This may occur if sexist, racist, or other offending terms are used.

Sexist Language. Language considered sexist will call attention to the speaker's method of expression rather than to ideas. Such language may also cause some listeners to reach un-

Fig. 3

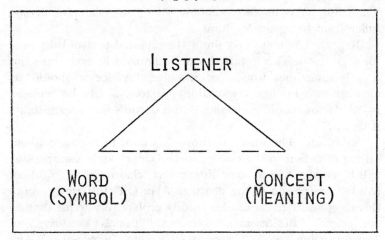

LISTENER

WORD
(SYMBOL)

CONCEPT
(MEANING)

Relationship of Words to Ideas

flattering conclusions about the speaker's fairmindedness and about the degree to which the speaker shows sensitivity to social concerns. The distractions of sexist language can easily be eliminated without creating another set of distractions based on clumsy nonsexist terms. The expression "unmanned boat" might well deflect the attention of some listeners. But the non-sexist "unpeopled boat" would probably distract even more. Saying "a boat with no one on board" would solve the problem without calling attention to the solution.

Avoiding the generic "man," eliminating terms such as "girls in the office," and not applying "he," "him," or "his" to a person of unknown sex can be accomplished by using a number of simple techniques.

Plural. The "he-his-him" problem can be readily solved by starting with a plural noun. Rather than saying "Whenever he can, an employee should add to his credit union account," a writer can choose "Whenever *they* can, employees should add to *their* credit union accounts." Using the plural will cause a slight loss of specificity, but if it is important in a particular case to make an example specific a person can be named. Either an actual or a hypothetical man or woman can be the subject of the example, which would then be specific without being sexist. The employee example used above, like many examples, doesn't suffer from being made plural.

Repeat. The noun may simply be repeated to avoid the need for a pronoun. This approach cannot be used in every case, but it will sometimes work. For instance, "A doctor should remember that his first responsibility is to. . ." can be replaced by "A doctor should remember that a doctor's first responsibility is to. . . ."

Substitute. The word "chairman" is hard to replace without calling attention to the change. Both "chair" and "chairperson" will be as offensive to some listeners as "chairman" is to others. (And "Chairperson of the Board of Ajax Oil" just won't work.) But most sexist terms can be readily replaced by terms that do not offend. "Businessman" becomes "business executive" or "person in business." "Housewife" becomes "homemaker." And "saleslady" becomes "salesperson." In the case of "unequal yoking" found in the expression "man and wife," either of the terms may be substituted to produce "husband and wife" or "man and woman."

Cut. Often the offending word may simply be edited out of a manuscript. "Lady lawyer" can be reduced to "lawyer," the "his" removed from "husband and his wife," and the "him" cut from "a citizen secure in the rights provided him by the constitution."

And/Or. The examples cited so far have been designed to remove sexism without calling attention to the change. There may be times when a deliberate reference to both sexes will be in order. Reference may then be made to "a soldier beginning his or her duties," "a speaker addressing his or her audience," or "an executive solving his or her problems." Officers of the International Association of Business Communicators, an organization with a membership more than fifty percent female, sometimes refer to a member in the abstract as "she or he." The use of "or" plus the reversal of the more common order of the two words serves to emphasize a speaker's intent to recognize the actual makeup of the membership.

Objections to removing sexism from language often include

ridiculous examples. "Personhole" for "manhole" or "woperson" for "woman" are sometimes cited as examples of changes needed to be consistent. If a writer remembers the semanticist's explanation of how meaning happens in communication, these examples are obviously absurd. The words "manhole" and "woman" in a proper context simply do not offend anyone. The words "girl" in reference to adult females, "his" in reference to a person of unspecified gender, or "wife" in the phrase "a husband and his wife" *do* offend a significant number of people. Changing such expressions does less to make a political or social statement than it does to achieve clarity by directing attention to ideas and not to the words used to express the ideas.

Racist and Other Offending Terms. Just as sexist words distract, so may words that offend ethnic groups or words that are considered derogatory by increasing numbers of people who identify with disabled persons or older citizens. The word "black" should therefore not be used in a negative sense, but should be cut or replaced by any of several words that will carry the desired meaning without the possibility of embarrassment.

Public awareness of the offensive implications of such terms as "cripple," "basket case," "deaf and dumb," and even "handicapped" has been relatively recent. Increasingly, however, more and more listeners in a wide variety of audiences will be sensitive to careless use of these words.

This discussion of words that distract is but an introduction to a complicated subject. The International Association of Business Communicators book, *Without Bias,* edited by Judy Pickens, and Miller and Swift's *The Handbook of Nonsexist Writing*—both publications are cited in the bibliography at the end of this book—explore the topics in more detail. The concern here has been limited to achieving clarity by avoiding distractions.

VIVID LANGUAGE

Words have the ability to evoke all of the human senses. A vivid description of a headache in an aspirin commercial seems designed to make a viewer hurt, and any detailed conversational account of a broken arm will have the same effect on most listeners. A glowing account of a good meal does in fact "make the mouth water" as words create an image almost real enough to appeal to the taste buds. The sense of smell and the sense of hearing are a bit harder to awaken with words, but any listener who has mowed a lawn or witnessed a thunderstorm may have the smells and sounds of those events brought back by a lively description of them in a speech.

The visual image is perhaps the most common and the most useful. A good description can transmit a picture to a listener's mind where it will stick. "The Iron Curtain" captures a concept so well with a picture that the phrase from a Churchill speech was added to the language of international politics. But a business speaker fixed an image in the mind of an audience with equal success by reminding it that before the days of the automobile, pollution from transportation came in the form of horse manure on the streets.

A good image in a speech must be worded with sufficient detail to permit the audience to "see" the picture. Color, size, shape, movement, and direction are among the elements that can be included. Karl Eller, President of Combined Communications Corporation, used a vivid description of milk production to illustrate the free enterprise system. Here is part of his image:

> I'm going to leave you with a little reminder. That reminder is a glass of milk. . . . But look at that milk and think about what it took to bring that glass of milk to your table. Some farmer bred and raised the cow. Some farmer owned and tended the land it grazed on. . . . Some farmer milked the cow or cows and sold the milk to someone else who processed it, pasteurized it and packaged it. . . . And all along the line the product was either made better or its distribution was simplified and narrowed and a lot of people had jobs. Wealth was created. Someone was paid to haul the milk to the restaurant and paid to carry it inside and put it in the refrigerator. The waitress was paid wages. . . . You order milk. You got milk. But you got more than milk. You got a miracle in a glass. The miracle of created wealth. [*Vital Speeches,* February 1, 1979, p. 232]

APPROPRIATE LANGUAGE

A passage composed for one speech may crop up in a later talk on the same general subject. Writers in an organization freely borrow from one another, so a section of one speech may be transferred to a talk by another speaker. A politician on a hectic schedule may deliver essentially the same message to several audiences. In each of the above instances, fine tuning of the language will often be required. It must be appropriate for each speaker, for each audience, and for each occasion.

President Franklin Roosevelt had an especially good ear for the right word on the right occasion. When Frances Perkins wrote for him, she included in a social security speech the line, "We are trying to construct a more inclusive society." When she heard the speech on her car radio, Roosevelt had changed the passage to read, "We are going to make a country in which no one is left out." At times Roosevelt knew the appropriate word should be more rather than less eloquent. When his writers presented him with a draft of his declaration of war address, one line read, "a date which will live in *history*." His change to the word "infamy" became one of the most famous examples of his ability to strike the appropriate note in a speech.

Russell Conwell delivered his lecture, "Acres of Diamonds," over five thousand times, but he adjusted it slightly for each audience. Modern writers need to recognize that while each speech does not have to be completely new, it must be adapted to fit the needs of the new situation. Choosing appropriate language will often make the difference between a good speech and a bad one.

SPECIAL CONSIDERATIONS IN LANGUAGE

PROBLEMS IN HEARING WORDS

The English language creates a few traps for the unwary speaker. Words that sound alike but have different meanings are instantly clear in print but not in speech. "The Jimmy Carter era" may, depending on the speaker's pronunciation, sound the same as "The Jimmy Carter error." "An expensive site" is heard by some as "an expensive sight." And the speaker who said of the woman he was introducing, "She and her entire family have this special something in their genes" did not realize that many people in his audience would hear the last word as "jeans."

The phrase "in sufficient numbers" may seem to some to be

"insufficient numbers." The list could be expanded to include "in adequate," "in appropriate," and "in sensible." The listener will correct the mistake when the context of the words become clear, but there will be a momentary problem.

Words difficult for the speaker to pronounce should be avoided. President Ford had the habit of adding an extra syllable to "judgment," and President Carter never seemed to master "nuclear." Almost any speaker will have trouble with tongue twisters where "r" and "w" sounds are put too close together or where a number of "s" sounds give the speech a hissing quality.

ATTRIBUTION OF QUOTES

In essays or reports, quotes are often written with the "he said" or "she said" in the middle to break up the monotony of the quotation. Sometimes the attribution appears at the end of the quote. Neither of these approaches works well in speaking. Here is a passage which, if read aloud, will show the problem:

> "You can never," he said, "make up your mind about anything."
> "Oh, I don't know about that," I replied.

In normal speech the exchange would read something like this:

> He said, "You can never make up your mind about anything," and I said, "Oh, I don't know about that."

For the most part, synonyms for "said" should be avoided, but at times such words as "noted," "pointed out," "observed," "contended," or "wrote" will help establish the tone of the material to be quoted. In humorous material especially writers will often find awkward substitutions for "said" in print: "he sputtered" or "he responded gamely." "Said" is almost always safer.

If a speaker has the ability to use vocal inflection to mark the quoted material, "said" can be—like "quote" and "unquote" —omitted altogether. "Let's see what Joe Jones had to say on that point" or "Here's Joe Jones's opinion."

While any quotation a speaker uses will necessarily have been made in the past, a convention in public speaking allows for use of the present tense. It may make a quotation sound slightly more dramatic to say "As Joe Jones puts it" or "Joe Jones writes in his new book that. . . ."

ZINGERS AND OTHER RHETORICAL DEVICES

The Zinger. Occasionally a writer may want to insert a few deliberate rhetorical devices into a speech. The zinger is a typical example. President Ford had a standard zinger he could insert as needed in speeches on political subjects. It was "And don't forget that a government big enough to give you everything you want is big enough to take away everything you have!" Jay Van Andel, speaking as Chairman of the United States Chamber of Commerce, used a variation on Ford's theme with a zinger that said, "Remember, when someone gets something for nothing, someone else gets nothing for something." [*Vital Speeches,* July 1, 1979, p. 556]

A zinger is a sort of rhetorical bumper sticker that makes a point in a clever, popular, and sometimes humorous manner. It usually involves obvious wordplay and it usually can be quoted without knowing the context of the speech. A sample somewhat longer than usual was delivered by Norman D. Potter of Cities Service Company at a State Jaycees meeting: "Scientists say that giants no longer walk the earth. They may be right, but Jaycees are leaving some mighty big footprints." [*Vital Speeches,* January 1, 1980, p. 181] In a short zinger, Congresswoman Shirley Chisholm said, "Not failure, but low aim, is sin." [*Vital Speeches,* August 15, 1978, p. 671]

Alliteration. A little alliteration can enliven a speech. If overdone—and the previous sentence approaches the boundary—it will annoy. Here is a phrase from an early draft of a speech that offers an excellent opportunity for adding alliteration: "Oil companies are making huge investments in modernizing refineries." The word "huge" should probably be replaced simply because it is a loaded word that should not appear in a sentence sympathetic to oil companies. Replacing it with "major"—a word with more positive connotations—permits a modest level of alliteration with "making" and "modernizing." The "m" sound in investments does not get enough stress to overdo the alliteration.

Alliteration may be used for words in a sequence of ideas or even in wording main points. Paul Wise, President of the Alliance of American Insurers, for example, developed a five-point speech on arson control using the words Commitment, Creativity, Credibility, Courage, and Coordination. [*Vital Speeches*, November 1, 1978, pp. 61-64]

Balance. The zingers by President Ford and Jay Van Andel illustrate balance in sentence structure. So does the "ask not" line from John F. Kennedy. As in the case of alliteration, this device must not be overused. If too many balanced sentences are included, a speech will have a sing-song sound. Also, balance should not be an end in itself; the form must not overcome substance as it did in the case of the protester carrying a sign reading "Power, yes. Power Plants, no."

The rhetorical devices discussed here are the most important of those available. But more may be used. Hyperbole, parallelism, and onomatopoeia are, among others, devices writers may try.

LOADED LANGUAGE

A professor of rhetoric once observed "language is sermonic." Words preach. The language used in discussion of social and political issues will seldom be neutral. Writers must have a sensitivity to loaded language. They should avoid using words loaded against the arguments they make, and they should choose the most positive terms available that will give honest support to their claims.

A writer for a corporation, for example, will find many terms in common use reflect negatively on business. To take a well-known example, the word "profit" should not appear in an incidental context in a business speech to the general public. Unless a speech discusses profit directly, casual references to the concept will frequently be made with such terms as "earnings" or "return on investment." Substitution solves the problem.

As an alternative to substitution, negatively loaded terms can be qualified when they are used. The term "consumer advocate," for instance, is a highly loaded phrase. It suggests someone standing up for the rights of *all* consumers even though some individuals who acquire the label represent only a small number of consumers. A business speaker who refers to such a person must qualify the term either directly by discussing the label or indirectly by prefacing it with a limiting phrase such as "so-called." Oil industry speakers, for example, routinely explain or qualify the term "windfall profits tax."

Where possible, negative terms should be replaced with positive ones. "Major investments" rather than "huge investments" illustrates this approach. A writer in the electric power field should not refer to higher rates during peak hours as "a penalty." The industry strategy for encouraging conservation would be better expressed by the word "incentive."

Another aspect of loaded language might be called the you-we-they problem. Almost never will a speaker get a fair hearing by saying, "The trouble is you are not working hard enough." To avoid creating a communication barrier, the speaker would have to move at least as far as the "we" on the scale and perhaps in some cases as far as the "they." However, it would not be wise to say, "Our customers [i.e., they] will benefit" when the speaker could say "You will benefit." Roughly speaking, "you" get the good news, "they" get the bad news, and "we" get the challenges.

When facing almost any tough issue, writers will discover that opposition speakers and writers take full advantage of the sermonic nature of language. Most speaking finds its justification in our society's advocacy approach to resolving problems; two sides debate and the public decides. If an argument is logical and honest, it should be stated in language that makes the case in the most positive manner possible.

CONCLUSION

No feature of speech writing presents a greater challenge to a writer's abilities than does language. The suggestions in this chapter highlight some of the problems writers face. The problems can be solved, not by an easy formula, but by hours of writing and rewriting.

CHAPTER VII

HUMOR

"The wit that suits the orator is rare." [Quintilian, Roman Teacher of Rhetoric]

The modern speech writer cannot afford to ignore the role of humor in communication. The demand for good humor in speeches has never been greater. For instance, many corporate officers are no longer willing to settle for a few tired jokes in opening a speech. They now insist on having the quality of humor they see not merely in entertainment but increasingly in outstanding business and political speeches.

As Bob Orben points out, "Humor has often been the key that unlocks an audience's receptivity." [Orben, p. 3] Orben, who once headed President Ford's speech writing staff, has written for Red Skelton, Jack Parr, and Dick Gregory. He takes humor seriously. In workshops he conducts for speakers and speech writers he finds a steady demand for his professional advice on choosing and using humor in speeches.

Speech writers can purchase publications offering current humor—Orben's *Current Comedy* is one excellent source cited in the bibliography—or they can buy tailor-made humor at prices that may range from a few hundred to a few thousand dollars. Not many speech writers will actually need to write original humor, but even that may be done by reworking a piece of humor or by creating humor with a standard formula such as the good news-bad news idea.

Whatever approach a writer takes, some thinking about humor will be advisable. That thinking should start with a consideration of some of the problems that must be confronted in adding humor to speeches.

PROBLEMS

First of all, a writer will have great difficulty knowing what an audience will consider funny. Even professional comedians

120

sometimes fail to get a laugh with material supplied by highly competent comedy writers. Most speech writers don't have a professional sense of comedy, and most of the speakers they write for are far from professional in the timing skills required in the delivery of humorous material.

Second, when humor does fail, the results can be devastating to the speaker and to the success of the remainder of the speech. The silence following the punch line will seem like an eternity. The only thing worse than complete silence would be the sound of the speaker laughing alone.

Third, humor, which often depends on an element of exaggeration and a willing suspension of disbelief, may be completely misunderstood. Some listeners will accept in dead seriousness an idea intended to be funny. This confusion is seen when a delightful piece of satire appears in a newspaper only to be followed a few days later by a letter to the editor from a reader who completely missed the point.

Fourth, some studies have found humor can cause speakers to lose credibility. This is a complicated matter, but it may be that a serious effort at persuasion will be jeopardized by innocent humor. Perhaps it was this problem that caused the nineteenth century U.S. Senator Tom Corwin to warn, "Never make people laugh. If you would succeed in life, you most be solemn as an ass. All the great monuments are built over solemn asses."

THE VALUE OF HUMOR IN SPEECHES

In spite of these problems, writers have a wide range of reasons for including a humorous touch in a speech. For one thing, the speaker may demand it. An adamant "Put me a couple of jokes in there" may settle the issue. Or the situation may call for humor, even if both speaker and writer would prefer to avoid it. If all the events preceding the speech take place in an atmosphere of fun and games, a speaker can hardly make an abrupt shift to somber material.

Of course, if humor succeeds in a speech, the payoff will be significant. Humor can help hold an audience's attention and can even revive a tired and listless group of listeners. A laugh or a smile produces an interaction with the speaker, and when something strikes them as funny, members of an audience often become more alert by looking at one another and responding to the reactions of others. As Quintilian expressed it in the first century A.D., the effect of humor on the listener is that of "diverting his mind from too intense application to the subject before it, recruiting at times its powers, and reviving it after disgust and fatigue." In other words, humor wakes up the audience.

Also, a light touch can go a long way in revealing a speaker's friendliness and good will. After he lost an important political battle, John F. Kennedy showed he was a good sport by telling a rather old joke. Kennedy said following his defeat he felt much like the Western pioneer who was shot full of arrows and left alone on the prairie: "It only hurts when I laugh."

Humor, properly used, can drive home a point. When Carl E. Reichardt, President of Wells Fargo, wanted to criticize excessive reliance on efforts to measure the money supply in making financial decisions, he used humor to attack the complex formulas based on "M-1A, M-B, M-2 [and] M-3." He said, "One group of economists contends that adding all these various types of transactions together to get a money supply figure is like adding roller skates, pogosticks, and subway trains to arrive at a total number for transportation vehicles in the U.S." [*Vital Speeches*, September 15, 1981, p. 730]

Thus, in spite of its problems, humor does have its place. Writers can benefit from the occasional use of humor if they understand its distinctive role in communication and if they follow a few basic precautions.

THE SPECIAL NATURE OF HUMOR IN COMMUNICATION

Some comparisons have already been made between speech humor and humor used by comedians. Humor by a stand-up comic on the Carson Show or the humor in a skit in a variety program have something in common with the humor found in speeches. But the fundamental purposes of the professional entertainer and the speaker differ sharply.

A speaker should not judge the success of humor in communication on the basis of the amount of the laughter it gets. That sort of measurement is appropriate for an entertainer. One professional humor writer has suggested a good comedy routine should generate five laughs a minute. The number of laughs along with their duration and volume gives us a ready means of knowing if a comedian is "truly funny." In fact, one comic has a clever bit in which he plaintively criticizes the "silent laughers" who, to be polite, place their hands over their mouths to keep their merriment from being audible.

We judge humor in a speech by a different standard. The amount of overt audience response does not matter as much as the effect of the humor on the total success of the speech. The writer needs to ask will humor attract and hold attention, will it make a point clear, will it help the audience see the speaker is a caring, friendly person? To achieve these results, smiles and chuckles may do the job as well or better than roars of laughter.

Humor in communication, then, cannot be viewed as an end in itself. This is not to say that humor can never be the major vehicle for an argument. Aristophanes attacked the philosophy of Socrates in theatrical comedy, Swift made social and political points with satire, and *Doonesbury*, like many comic strips before it, uses biting humor to take sides on current events.

But if the listener or reader feels the humorist steps out of the bounds of the medium, there may be trouble. *Doonesbury* offers an interesting modern example. Some newspapers refuse to run the strip on the comics page because it argues while it entertains. An equally ambiguous case can be seen in the occasional controversy over a message behind the situations in which the TV character Archie Bunker is placed.

Strange as it may sound, *Doonesbury* and Archie Bunker succeed in walking a fine line *because most people do not take them seriously.* And this is a situation in which a writer does not want to place a speaker. If humor in a speech is excessive, if it is perceived as an end and not a means, the speaker has become a comic. In that role arguments lose their punch—*Gulliver's Travels* becomes mere entertainment and Archie Bunker's escapades don't change people's attitudes about racism. Senator Corwin's statement that monuments are built over "solemn asses" was an irrepressibly comic reflection of his belief that his heavy-handed use of jokes had adversely affected his political career.

Types of Humor

All too often writers and speakers think of humor as being limited to jokes. The joke, or humorous anecdote, is but one of the types of humor available. It has its place, but it should not be overused.

The Humorous Anecdote

Jimmy Durante used to say, "Everybody wants to get into the act." Ordinary people get into the comedy act with jokes. Children bring them home from school, adults tell them at parties and at the office. Anyone can tell a joke and everyone is a critic. That is both the strength and the weakness of jokes in speeches. Audiences find the joke a comfortable, familiar form of humor, but because they have heard and told so many—including the bad ones—a speaker faces a difficult assignment when called on to deliver a joke.

Introducing a humorous story in a speech can create a problem. In setting up a joke, the old "a funny thing" approach should be avoided. Any claim that the joke will be funny puts the audience in a "show me" frame of mind. "That reminds me" makes an equally weak beginning. The joke should be introduced without any special fanfare. It should begin the same as any other supporting material in the speech.

Three fairly typical jokes suitable for speeches appear below. With one exception they start out well. But because the jokes have not been adequately edited for the ear, they contain the following problems: (1) the punch lines are sometimes cluttered with extra words at the end, (2) clauses interrupt the flow of some of the sentences, (3) awkward sounding synonyms for "said" are used in some cases, (4) the placement of attribution of quoted words is in the wrong place, and (5) some of the language is for the eye and not the ear.

Each joke will be presented in its "print version" and then shown as it might be edited for the ear.

> I try to keep in mind the story about Frankie Albert, the former 49er football player, who was speaker at a father-and-son dinner. After the speech, he answered all questions thrown at him by the kids. One boy kept raising his hand until he caught Frankie's eye.

"And what's your question, sonny?" asked Albert.
"What's next on the program?" the kid said.

Here is an oral version:

I try to keep in mind the story about the former 49er football player Frankie Albert. He was once giving a speech at a father-and-son dinner, and after the speech he agreed to answer any questions the kids wanted to ask. One boy kept raising his hand until finally Frankie saw him and said, "And what's your question, sonny?"
The kid said, "What's next on the program?"

The biggest problem in the written version of this story is the placement of the attribution on the punch line. The phrase, "the kid said," comes at the point the audience should begin to laugh; it "steps on" the laughter. In the oral version, one clause has been eliminated (line 2) and the slightly difficult "asked Albert" has been altered.

Printed version of another example:

One of old coach George Halas's funniest stories has as its hero the Chicago Bear immortal, tackle George Musso. One afternoon Musso was flattened by a terrific block. The trainer dashed onto the field, while a stretcher crew poised for action on the sidelines.
When the trainer reached Musso, he found him just regaining consciousness. "How do you feel?" the trainer asked anxiously.
"Okay," replied the huge tackle. "But how's the crowd taking it?"

Oral version:

One of old coach George Halas's stories has as its hero the great Chicago Bear tackle George Musso. One afternoon Musso was knocked out cold by a terrific block. The trainer ran out on the field, and a stretcher crew on the sidelines was ready for action.
When the trainer got to Musso, he found him just coming to, and he said, "How do you feel?"
Musso said, "I'm okay, but how's the crowd taking it?"

This joke, alone of samples shown here, promises in the opening line of the original version that it will be funny. In addition, it puts the attribution either in the middle or at the end of the quoted words rather than at the start. And it has some words and phrases that look good in print but do not sound as conversational as required by a joke. For example, few people in conversation would say "the trainer dashed onto the field." Also, spoken humor does not need the word "anxiously" to explain how the trainer asked his question. The speaker's voice should convey the anxiety; if the emotion is not in the speaker's voice, the term "anxiously" will only make matters worse.

Printed version:

We've been like the hound dog in an Ozark story. The hound was sitting in a country store and howling his head off. A stranger came in and said to the storekeeper, "What's the matter with that howlin' dog?"

"He's sittin' on a cockleburr," said the storekeeper.

"Why doesn't he get off?" the stranger asked.

"He'd rather howl," came the answer.

Oral version:

We've been like the hound dog in an Ozark story. The hound was sitting in a country store howling his head off. A stranger came in and said to the storekeeper, "What's the matter with that howlin' dog?"

The storekeeper said, "He's sittin' on a cockleburr."

The stranger said, "Why doesn't he get off?"

The storekeeper shook his head and said, "He'd rather howl."

This anecdote has only two problems with its language. The first is, once again, with attribution. That can be solved by moving the attribution to the beginning of the sentences. The second problem comes with "setting up" the punch line. The four pieces of the dialogue come too quickly and too evenly for the punch line to stand out in the printed version. This is no problem to the reader who *sees* where the punch line falls on the page. But listeners need to *hear* the build up that lets them know the end is coming. If the speaker has the ability to handle it, the last three attributions could be eliminated altogether, leaving only the dialogue to carry the humor.

The three jokes above have been rewritten and examined in detail because they are fairly typical of the jokes writers find in print and transfer into speeches with too little editing. Many writers seem to treat a printed joke as though it were a quotation or a statistic—something that the writer has no authority to alter. That attitude should not prevail in using jokes; they must often be rewritten to suit the demands of oral style.

The Cover Line. When a speaker delivers the punch line in a joke, a crucial point has been reached. Bob Orben points out that an inexperienced speaker may not wait long enough for the audience to respond. Orben recommends that, rather than rushing on after a pause of a second or two, the speaker should attempt to force a laugh by waiting. He also suggests having a few quips or "savers" ready to turn the failure of a joke into a laugh. [Costello, p. 42] Johnny Carson is, of course, a modern master at getting a good laugh with a quick comment on the failure of a joke.

Writers can help speakers cope with potential failure by providing a cover line after a joke. The cover line can be especially valuable for speakers who must follow the manuscript closely because they cannot or will not ad-lib. A cover line comes immediately after the punch line. It consists of a brief comment on the joke, and it can serve either of two functions. If the joke gets a good reaction, the cover line will be perceived as a response to the audience's appreciation of the humor. If the joke dies, the cover line both justifies the joke that didn't prove to be funny and serves as a bridge from the wreckage of the joke back to the body of the speech.

A cover line for the Frankie Albert joke might be, "You have to admire honesty even when it hurts." This cover line would be almost a throwaway if it came following gales of laughter or a few dozen broad smiles. In those cases it would be saying, "We all understand kids, don't we?" But the line would be much more valuable if the joke got only blank stares from the listeners. Then the line would say, "Here is why I told you that story" and would permit the speaker to move on.

A cover line for the Musso story might be, "Now, that's what I'd call loyalty to the fans" and for the Ozark story, "I guess we've all run into that attitude before." Naturally, the content of the cover line depends on the point being made in the joke and the next idea in the speech. While not every speaker—or every joke—requires a cover line, the device may come in handy when a writer thinks a speaker may need an avenue of escape.

THE ONE-LINER

In many respects the "one-liner" is a much better vehicle for humor than the joke. The one-liner makes the humorous point quickly. Even though the term "one-liner" is a misnomer and this form of humor may consist of two or three sentences, it still does not require the involved build-up needed in jokes. It fits the fast pace of modern times.

When President Carter stated publicly "I'll whip his ass" in reference to his campaign against Ted Kennedy, the one-line response from Kennedy was "I knew the President was behind me, but I didn't know how close." Kennedy won the exchange even if not the nomination.

Abraham Lincoln often expressed an idea with a one-liner. When one of the several inept generals he appointed was asked where his headquarters was to be, the general replied, "My headquarters will be in the saddle." Lincoln at once recognized that the general had more style than ability and observed, "He's got his headquarters where his hindquarters ought to be."

Bob Orben wrote during one of the periods of heightened public concern over fuel supplies, "If God had wanted us to have gasoline, he wouldn't have given us the Department of Energy." The line was quoted in the *Wall Street Journal,* picked up by an oil company for an advertisement, and appeared in various forms in numerous speeches.

A one-liner can be an excellent substitute for the joke many speakers feel they need at the beginning of a speech. Beginning a talk before the Economic Club of Detroit, Howard M. Love, President of National Steel, said, "I remind myself that the secret to survival for speakers at The Economic Club of Detroit is similar to the secret to survival of the pedestrian in downtown Detroit traffic . . . there are the quick . . . and the dead. I plan to be quick!" [*Vital Speeches,* January 15, 1981, p. 216]

INTEGRATED HUMOR

Although both the one-liner and the joke may carry a

message, humor is their dominant element. First and foremost the speaker seeks to say something funny. Integrated humor reverses the roles of humor and substance. This type of humor states an idea in a clever way, but the idea dominates the humor. Unlike either the joke or the one-liner, the idea in integrated humor should be strong enough to stand on its own.

Richard G. Capen of Knight-Ridder Newspapers told a college audience he thought it a tragedy when someone achieves a career goal "and then looks back to wonder whether the trip was worth the price. Some such individuals find that they have climbed ladders propped up against the wrong walls." [*Vital Speeches,* October 1, 1980, p. 766]

Peter G. Peterson, Chairman of Lehman Brothers Kuhn Loeb, explained the difficulty Americans have in understanding some foreign countries by saying, "The Third World has always been what in the Nixon Administration we called a MEGO subject ('mine eyes glaze over') in terms of U.S. domestic politics." [*Vital Speeches,* December 15, 1980, p. 137]

Using the notion of eyes glazing over in another context, Judd H. Alexander, Senior Vice President of American Can, found integrated humor helpful in a speech on his industry's view of solid waste disposal problems. Explaining his troubles communicating with the Environmental Protection Agency, he said, "Were you ever in a restaurant, impatient to place your order, and you call over an idle waiter only to have him refuse to help by saying, 'it is not my table?' I have the same feeling when I try to describe the wonders and benefits of paper and packaging to E.P.A. officials. Their eyes glaze over because I am not at their table. I am talking communications and distribution and their table is garbage." [*Vital Speeches,* February 1, 1979, p. 252]

Mr. Alexander did not tell a joke. He did not, in the ordinary sense of the term, use a one-liner. He simply illustrated his point with a humorous idea cleverly worded. His content and his humor were thoroughly integrated. This type of humor offers extremely low risk to the speaker because if it were not funny at all, it would still support the speaker's case. Of course, there is every reason to expect that a non-hostile audience would find the story quite funny.

POEMS, PUNS, AND PRANKS

Poems. It is hard to say what has killed poetry in our society. One good explanation may be that the parent slowly smothered the child as poets over the years have grown increasingly more obscure. At any rate, the good has gone down with the bad, and even the delightful comic verse of the Ogden Nash and Richard Armour type is out of vogue. Almost all good limericks are too dirty to use in public, and the humor in the lyrics of popular songs is usually not intentional. So, the speech writer has little material available, and few audiences are attuned to humor in verse.

Occasionally, however, a poem can help make a point with a touch of humor. Grace J. Fippinger, Vice President, New York Telephone, recalled a few lines from Oliver Wendell Holmes to poke gentle fun at criticism:

> Whenever God sculpts an artist
> He gathers the chips that fall
> And out of them sculpts the critic,
> And that should explain it all.
> [*Vital Speeches,* January 15, 1980, p. 224]

Puns. Almost never can a writer include a pun in a speech. A speech with a pun would almost certainly have to be intended purely for entertainment in a situation such as a "roast." Puns invite groans, and speakers should not be deliberately exposed to a negative audience response. The temptation to use a pun may arise, but it should be suppressed.

Pranks. Again, except for highly specialized speeches, few opportunities arise for a speaker to use unusual dress, pratfalls, or comic visual aids to get laughter. Perhaps in an in-house safety talk a stooge might be brought in covered with fake bandages and a leg cast. Or to lighten a fund-raising talk a chart might depict a dollar bill being stretched or squeezed. But the opportunities for such unconventional devices are rare. They usually exist with "in" groups, and they depend on having a speaker who can avoid turning into a buffoon.

Using a professional magician or a clown to make a presentation may be effective, but it involves a type of communication beyond the scope of the present subject.

The distinctions among the types of humor discussed here may sometimes be hard to recognize. A long one-liner may be very much like a joke. If a writer quotes Mr. Alexander's story about the E.P.A., a piece of integrated humor will have become an anecdote. The point here, however, has not been to construct perfect classifications. The mechanics of classifying are less important than recognition of a great variety of available humor. Writers will find it especially valuable to remember that humor extends beyond the joke.

TESTS FOR HUMOR

Before any type of humor finds its way into a speech, it should pass three tests.

IS THE HUMOR RELEVANT?

All too many speakers begin with a few jokes and then say, in effect, "Now that the humor is over, I'll give my speech." Even if the jokes are funny, the audience's attention has been gained with a false start, and some listeners may feel they have been misled.

Equally bad is the speaker who abruptly says, "That reminds me of. . . ." and then wedges unrelated humor into a talk. Humor should be an integral part of a speech. It should clarify an idea or emphasize a point. Al Capp, for example, was making an argument when he said that a college president who thinks the students are better able to run the school than the president, is probably right.

IS THE HUMOR IN GOOD TASTE?

A study of the history of humor bears out what anyone knows who hears jokes on the job. Vulgarity and cruelty appear with regularity in humor. These two features supply much of the "shock value" needed to make some humor work.

The difference between the private telling of offensive humor and its exposure in public can be seen in the widely-publicized jokes told a few years back by former cabinet officer Earl Butz. His jokes were no worse than those told every day in offices and at parties, but once they were revealed to the public there was a roar of protest. On a much smaller scale, a speech writer should remember that a joke that depends for its humor on having a fat man in it will not necessarily sound offensive in the office. But when the speaker begins to read the joke to an audience and notices three stout people in the front row, the speaker and the audience will both be embarrassed.

A growing number of groups have increasing consciousness of their identity accompanied by an increased sensitivity to being the target of humor. Gray awareness and gay awareness are but two current examples. To be safe, only Blacks can tell jokes about Blacks, and the right to poke fun at school teachers should be reserved to those who teach school.

Only recently have efforts been made to measure possible negative effects on speakers who use self-disparaging humor. One such study examined the impact on an audience when speakers explained the value of their professions but in the process used humor that had those professions as its target. One of the speeches defended the field of economics while including deprecating humor such as the one-liner, "If all economists were laid end to end, they would still each point in a different direction." [Chang and Gruner, p. 421]

The study found no significant negative reaction to the selfdisparaging humor. The authors did, however, suggest two precautions with humor of this sort. They warn that the humor may not be successful unless the audience has a high degree of respect for the speaker. They also caution that in the process of the speaker disparaging the speaker's own group, no strongly held beliefs of the audience should be at the same time held up to ridicule.

So, humor at the speaker's expense seems safe. For example, Richard Nixon used a self-deprecating remark as he started to rebuild his political fortunes following his 1960 series of television confrontations with John F. Kennedy. Recognizing that Kennedy's performance helped decide the election, Nixon quipped, "I'm a dropout from the electoral college. I flunked debate."

Is the Humor Fresh?

Those who say there's no such thing as a new joke may be right. After all, most humor fits into a few basic formulas. Humor has a way of spreading quickly over a wide region, going through a dormant period, and then cropping up again.

Since speech writers do not often create humor but rather adapt existing material, they need to be especially concerned about the problem of using stale wit. A stale joke is not the same thing as an old joke. A good story from the current *Reader's Digest* is likely to be "stale" because so many people have heard or read it. A piece of humor from a two-year old copy of the *Digest* will be "old" but possibly quite usable.

Here is a sample of humor which could easily be updated to apply in the conflict between the Poles and the Russians in the 1980s. The story was widely told in the early 1950s. The dialogue takes place between a Communist official and a pupil from a Polish school:

> "Who is your father?"
> "Stalin, the father of all progress."
> "Very good, and who is your mother?"
> "The Soviet Union, mother of all peace-loving people."
> "Splendid! Now, tell me, my little fellow. What would you like to be when you grow up?"
> "An orphan."

One way to meet the need for fresh humor is to draw material from the speaker's personal or business experience. Almost everyone has a collection of "funny things that happened to me" stories. These incidents are usually not clever enough to be sold to the *Digest*, but their weaknesses are compensated for by the fact that they really happened.

In a speech expressing concern over growing "technicalization" of society, New York University Professor Neil Postman used a humorous personal story to complain about our reliance on numerical scores to reflect concepts that can't truly be measured:

> Because I had received an 83 in English, I had missed by a fraction being eligible for Arista, the high school equivalent of making the Dean's List. I therefore approached my English teacher, a gentle and sensitive man by the name of Rosenbaum, and requested that he reassess my performance with a view toward elevating my grade two points. He regarded my request as reasonable and studiously examined his record book. Then he turned toward me with genuine sadness in his face and said, "I'm sorry, Neil. You're an 83.

An 84 at most, but not an 85. Not this term, anyway." [*Vital Speeches,*
January 1, 1979, p. 183]

The President of New York Telephone, Mr. D. C. Staley,
found a story from his experience valuable in the opening of a
speech:

> They tell the story of a Bell System executive who showed up for
> a speaking occasion. As he approached the banquet hall, someone
> called out—"The telephone man is here." The hotel manager, stand-
> ing nearby, turned to an assistant and said, "That was fast. Show
> him where to install it."
> That may sound like telephone fiction—but I want you to know
> that I missed out on the prime ribs that day. [*Vital Speeches,* No-
> vember 1, 1980, p. 39]

The effort to personalize humor should not extend to lying.
Often a speaker will say something like "There was this Baptist
preacher in my home town. . . ." and then go on to tell a standard
borrowed joke. This practice runs the risk of undermining the
speaker's credibility. It should not be used unless the speaker is
confident the audience will know from the beginning the story
should not be taken at face value.

SOURCES OF HUMOR

Speech writers who use humor should keep a file of good
material. Such a file will help cut down on the frustration of
facing a deadline for a speech while plowing through page after
page in a published collection of humor. It is unreasonable to
expect a quick search to produce suitable humor from such a
source. Any humor collection must be broad enough to appeal
to thousands of readers; naturally it can not contain a high per-
centage of jokes that suit the needs of any one individual.

The few useful bits from a collection should be culled out
and filed separately with a good index. Into this system should
go the clever items gathered from non-humor sources such as
news stories, magazine articles, and books. (Watch for headlines
such as the one proclaiming "Senators for Sale" over a story
announcing that two senators were in support of weapons sales
to a foreign government.) By working over a period of time to
select only the material relevant to a writer's needs, the search

process can be shortened in those crucial hours before a speech draft is due.

Humor can be borrowed from other speeches. It can be jotted down after an amusing incident has occurred in the office. It can be taken from graffitti, bumper stickers, T-shirts, cartoons, comic strips, and comedians on TV or radio. And it can be bought from professional writers and compilers of humor.

Oben's *Current Comedy* has already been mentioned. This collection of one-liners over a period of time will yield a large reservoir of appropriate humor. An excellent, if somewhat unusual, source is the compilation of humor from major newspapers sold by Mack McGinnis. Outstanding current humor can be gleaned from his bi-monthly publication, and McGinnis also has available from his collection back files of humor catalogued under various headings.

Recorded speeches on humor and humorous topics by Art Fettig and Mick Delaney provide writers with material as well as with ideas on the effective use of humor.

Fettig makes the point that skill in using humor can be cultivated. The art of humor requires work and study. The above suggestions set forth the basics. Observation and experience take over after that.

CHAPTER VIII

PRESENTATION OF THE SPEECH

"Gentlemen, reading from speeches is a very tedious business, particularly for an old man who has to put on spectacles, and more so if the man be so tall that he has to bend over to the light." [Abraham Lincoln, Speech in Chicago, July 10, 1858]

In discussing the presentation of a speech, writer Mike Stott compares a speech writer to a caddy for a pro golfer. The caddy suffers through every bad shot and rejoices in every good one. And a caddy, like a writer, has to be prepared to offer sound advice. The writer, of course, has one important limitation that the caddy doesn't. The writer can make suggestions only during the practice rounds or in the clubhouse afterwards. In actual delivery, speakers are on their own.

To carry the comparison between the golfer and the speaker one step further, control of physical behavior is of vital importance to both. However much a speaker might like to believe that the words of a speech will get the message over without regard to how the speaker performs, the fact remains that audiences pay a great deal of attention to what speakers do as well as what they say.

IMPORTANCE OF PRESENTING A SPEECH WELL

In everyday communication most people actually put more weight on the *how* than on the *what*. When a parent asks a child "Did you break this lamp?" the words in the child's answer will get much less attention than the child's wavering eye movement, shifting posture, and unsteady tone of voice. Although listeners don't often articulate the standards of judgment they apply, they do carefully study how messages are delivered in both casual conversation and in formal speeches.

Some people develop annoying habits that distract from their words. Nervous mannerisms, aimless motions, or monoto-

136

nous vocal tone may replace ideas as the focal point of a listener's attention. Yet somehow large numbers of speakers have risen to important positions requiring a great deal of public speaking, without having been told something as simple as "you really shouldn't scratch yourself *there* when giving a talk."

The emphasis should not all be on the negative. A speaker with ringing conviction in the voice can add a valuable dimension to the words on the page. Determination can be shown in facial expression, posture, and gesture far better than it can be stated in words. The presentation of the speech should not be considered a dull chore that must be done out of necessity; it is rather an opportunity to bring the ideas of a speech to life.

In order to see a speech presented to best advantage—and to avoid the agony of watching the labor of many hard hours of work destroyed—a speech writer may need to play the role of speech coach. Good coaching starts with understanding the fundamentals of effective speech delivery. These fundamentals can be reduced to a few simple but crucial points on proper management of voice and bodily action.

PRINCIPLES OF DELIVERY

CONTACT WITH THE AUDIENCE

Unless a speaker interacts with an audience, the message of the speech might just as well be delivered by tape recorder or even printed and mailed to its recipients. Eye contact between speaker and listener makes interaction possible. A speaker must look at—and see—the people in an audience if the feeling of a live presentation is to be preserved.

In conversation or in speaking from notes, a speaker has the valuable opportunity to adjust to audience responses—to add, to restate, to change direction. A speaker holding to the language of a manuscript lacks that flexibility, but will nevertheless find eye contact beneficial.

Eye contact helps hold attention. Listeners are less likely to talk to one another, to sleep, or to read a newspaper if the speaker periodically gets free of the text long enough to look at them. Eye contact will also give the speaker clues about the delivery of the speech. Someone straining to hear, for example, makes it obvious that the speaker needs to get closer to the mike or project the voice better. Signs of restlessness tell the speaker to move, gesture, or even pause to regain attention.

Often speakers will see signs of vigorous agreement or disagreement that tempt them to leave the safety of the manuscript and adjust the content of a speech in recognition of the response. Only highly skilled speakers can leave the page, add new material, and return to the manuscript smoothly. Most find it extremely difficult to make a logical transition back to the text, and even if they do so successfully the digression will add to the length of what was once a carefully-timed speech. With thorough audience analysis, there should be relatively little need for digressions.

While most speakers would be better off if they did not make significant alterations during delivery, some minor changes may prove useful. Occasionally, a controversial passage may be marked to indicate the speaker should leave it in if the audience is responding well but take it out if the audience reacts negatively to earlier parts of the talk. And small asides such as "I see Joe Jones agrees with that approach" may enliven a talk.

Techniques. Eye contact must be real if it is to be of any value. Furtive glances at the back wall or blank looks at the spaces between listeners will not be helpful. With practice, almost any speaker can learn to pick up a sentence or a long phrase with a quick look and then deliver it directly to the audience.

The first line in the above paragraph, for example, can be absorbed at a glance and then said without looking back down. That particular sentence would, in normal speech, take about four seconds to deliver. While it is being said, a speaker could establish meaningful eye contact with two people for two seconds each. By looking each person directly in the eye, the speaker could assure their continued attention (or jolt them back into attention) and at the same instant get a quick reading on how well the speech is being received.

Typing a manuscript in proper form can help a speaker use eye contact more freely. The type should be large, of course, and only about the upper half or two-thirds of the page should be used. This will avoid giving the audience a view of the top of the speaker's head as the speaker follows the text to the very bottom. Also, lines should never be broken at the end of a page. There are many reasons for this, including the fact that it often creates artificial pauses when the page must be turned, but it has the particular advantage of making the last line easy to pick up and deliver with good eye contact. After all, one of the speaker's major problems will be returning to the correct line after eye contact; if that line is the first one on the next page, the transition will be easy.

Some one-sentence paragraphs can be used. Such a paragraph, especially on the double spaced page of a manuscript, can be easily picked up.

A "zinger" might be colored with a highlight pen both to help the speaker scoop it up in one glance and to indicate clearly where the reading of the text will resume. Or a line might be arranged on the page with attention to units of thought rather than to grammatical structure as can be seen by rearranging the previous sentence in this paragraph:

A "zinger" might be colored with a highlight pen

both to help the speaker scoop it up in one glance

and to indicate clearly

where the reading of the text will resume.

One of the safest techniques for returning to the text after eye contact happens also to be the simplest. The speaker looks a member of the audience directly in the eye, perhaps while gesturing forcefully with the left hand, and then picks up the next words at the point where the index finger of right hand has been firmly planted. Speakers who were broken of this habit in the first grade will be able to relearn it with a little practice.

A speaker should not wear a deadpan expression when making eye contact. Almost every speech has its light moments where a smile is appropriate, its moments when a look of concern or alarm or satisfaction are in order. No speaker should be expected to take a short course in acting to show simple emotions through facial expression. But speakers should be reminded of the need to react normally in establishing eye contact. A speaker who habitually faces the public with a scowl (reflecting the speaker's discomfort rather than any ideas in the speech) may actually find it easier to use normal facial expressions when eye contact is made, not with the lifeless manuscript, but with live human beings in an audience.

POSTURE

A speaker will normally need a lectern to hold the manuscript, and even a speaker with access to an elaborate video prompting mechanism will usually be expected to stand half hidden behind what will ordinarily be a heavy mass of polished wood. If the speaker succumbs to the temptation to lean on or brace against the lectern, a barrier to communication will have been created.

A speaker draped over a lectern does not present the image desired in most speeches. The posture of such a speaker suggests uncertainty and unsteadiness.

A speaker should be advised to stand free and clear of the lectern with weight balanced almost equally on each foot. This posture projects an image that is "square," "solid," and "alert."

Speakers should aim for a posture of "relaxed attention." The shoulders should be level. Without being excessively rigid, the back should be straight and the head up. While audiences are seldom conscious of the details of posture, a speaker twisted into a pretzel position will send a subtle, nonverbal message that at the subconscious level advises the listener not to take this speaker seriously.

GESTURE

For some reason many people are self-conscious and even embarrassed about their gestures. "People tell me I talk with my hands" seems almost a confession of guilt. The fact of the matter is that gestures are helpful in communication. They serve a variety of useful functions.

Gestures emphasize. The thrusting index finger may be the most emphatic gesture, but a number of movements from the two-handed chopping motion to the pounding of the fist help a speaker signal "now hear this, this idea is important."

Gestures describe. Movement of the hands can show direction, size, and shape. When speakers talk of something large or small, fast or slow, up or down, or straight or crooked, gestures naturally supplement the words of the speech.

Gestures signal. From the obvious use of a "thumbs up" or "we're number one" to the more subtle open-handed gesture accompanying a plea for help, many gestures have acquired a generally accepted meaning in a given society.

Gestures relieve tension. Most speakers feel more at ease after they have made a few gestures. The movement expends some of the pent-up nervousness that goes along with speaking.

Gestures attract attention. A motionless speaker usually has little more appeal to the eye than any other lifeless object before the audience. The motion of a gesture can attract the attention of an audience.

Rules for Using Gestures. Preplanned or "canned" gestures almost always look odd. That is because the timing is usually off. A gesture ordinarily comes at the very moment an idea is being emphasized, described, or otherwise supported by a gesture. It may precede the idea slightly in some cases. But canned gestures tend to come a split second late, and they almost always appear ludicrous. Speakers should attempt in rehearsal of a talk to find places where a gesture feels natural rather than arbitrarily to insert a few where the writer thinks the speech needs some help.

Many speakers who gesture with vigor in normal conversation will make tiny motions while speaking. These motions cannot be seen by most listeners, and if they are seen, they appear quite out of place. Speakers should be aware of the need to get gestures free of the lectern so they will not be blocked from the audience's view.

What to Do With the Hands. It can be amusing to watch a speaker search for places to bring hands to rest when they are not in motion. The lectern is sometimes gripped tightly or the hands may travel about the body searching for a landing place. To the amusement of some in an audience, a speaker may resort to the "fig leaf" position with hands clasped at arms length in front of the body.

There are three comfortable positions for hands when they

are not performing some useful service such as gesturing or turning a page.

They may hang normally at the sides. Many speakers find this feels odd at first, and they need to be reassured that it looks quite normal. There is nothing wrong with one or both hands in the pockets if the result is casual and not strained—and if the pockets allow for the hands to fit comfortably. Or hands may rest lightly on the lectern. So long as the speaker does not put any weight on them or cling to the sides of the stand with them, this arrangement places the hands in a convenient place from which to launch a gesture.

VOICE

The Drone. Monotony in voice results from excessive regularity in pitch and rate. The solution does *not* come from giving the speaker advice on manipulating the melody and alternating the speed of the voice. This would quite likely produce an odd sing-song effect as bad as the original problem. The speaker should be encouraged to think of the speech, not as a sequence of words, but as a sequence of ideas. As was mentioned in the discussion of eye contact, a number of ways of arranging and marking the phrases on the manuscript may help break up excessive monotony.

The Racer. Many speakers speed up when they think a speech is going badly. This usually results in making the speech even worse than the speaker thought it was. The suggestion to slow down is a rather simple one compared to the complicated manipulations of the voice required in avoiding monotony. Therefore most speakers are able to monitor their rate and reduce it once the problem comes to their attention.

In addition to simply slowing the number of words per minute in a passage, a speaker can also take advantage of the pause. Some speech writers include the instructions "(PAUSE)" in the manuscript at appropriate places. Other writers use double or triple slash marks or extra space between paragraphs. The speaker should be comfortable with whatever solution is employed.

The Pontificator. Faced with a microphone or an audience, it is natural to feel that the normal speaking voice is not impressive enough. But speakers should avoid trying for an abnormally low pitch and an impressive but strained vocal quality. Large numbers of people do not like the sounds of their own voices, but except in extraordinary cases audiences soon adjust to the sound the speaker makes. Therefore, speakers should not attempt to mimic the vocal timbre of professional actors or announcers. Such an effort will produce strain along with an artificiality that can distract a listener.

The Inaudible. If a microphone is required in order to be heard, it should be properly adjusted before the speaker begins to talk, and the speaker should speak, not to the mike, but through it to the audience. Depending on the capability of the equipment, the speaker's movement in the delivery of the speech may be severely limited.

If at all possible, a microphone should not be used. A speaker should be advised to project or "aim" the voice at the farthest person in the room. It is usually *not* a good idea to suggest that a speaker "talk louder." This may result in strain.

COACHING THE SPEAKER

Not even a skilled, experienced speaker can expect to deliver a speech well without practice. For any important speech, the speaker should have a dress rehearsal with the writer present. All elements of the actual speech should be duplicated as far as is practical. The speech should be read as many times as it takes for the speaker to be comfortable with it.

A few days before the dress rehearsal, it may be helpful to have a "dry run." This could be especially valuable if complicated visuals are to accompany the speech. Even if the visuals are not fully ready, the dry run begins to acquaint the speaker with the talk and with how it will be presented.

Opinions differ on the sources to which a speaker should turn for counsel on the techniques of delivery. Getting advice from family members or colleagues without professional backgrounds in communication can present problems. A speaker who comes back to the office with a collection of bad suggestions from a spouse or a friend puts the speech writer in an awkward position.

But most speakers do need coaching and the writer should

seek to conduct it or at the very least to control it. The only people present at a practice session should be those who know enough about speech presentation to make intelligent suggestions and who will be candid in their remarks.

RECORDING THE PRACTICE SESSION ON VIDEO TAPE

A critique of a speaker's dry run and dress rehearsal will be especially valuable if recorded on video, but care must be taken to use the practice session to its fullest advantage.

A studio setting should be avoided. Technicians tampering with lights and mike will only serve to distract the speaker. The simplest kind of camera available should be used with normal room lighting, and the microphone should be adjusted before the practice begins (with no interruption at the start of the speech caused by the need to attach a mike to the speaker's clothing). The setting should be a conference room or large office. The key word for the operator of the equipment is "unobtrusive."

After the practice run has been recorded and before viewing the tape, the speech writer should get the speaker engaged in a discussion of the effectiveness of the presentation. It will be useful to have two pads or two chalkboard sections on which key performance points can be listed.

The critique should begin by listing the positive features of the presentation. The speaker may wish to dwell on the negative, but an effort should be made to itemize first the aspects of the practice that went well. The writer should add to the list as the discussion progresses. If others have been invited to take part in the critique, they can be asked for comments after the speaker has had the opportunity to contribute.

The video does not catch everything of importance; for example, it is quite difficult to tell much about eye contact from the tape. The picture will show only if the speaker is looking down or not; it will not show if eye contact was made with a listener. Position of the feet, which may affect posture, will usually be left out of the picture.

The second list should be made up of "features which can be improved." In conducting a critique, the greatest care must be taken both to report honestly on the areas of needed improvement and to avoid wounding the speaker's feelings. Speaking is a personal matter; the ego is involved. Therefore, descriptions of weaknesses in delivery should not be discussed with such terms as "bad," "weak," or "unsatisfactory." If eye contact does not appear adequate, "more" should be called for. If the gestures are too small, the writer's recommendation should again be in positive language with the suggestion that "they should be up higher and more obvious to the audience." Distracting mannerisms can be discussed with such terms as "can be avoided" or "does not add to the effectiveness of the speech."

This is not to suggest that a good critique overlooks areas of weakness. These areas should be made obvious. Most speakers, who after all can see the problems for themselves when viewing the tape, appreciate having specific suggestions made. A surprising number of such speakers are surrounded by advisors who lack the courage to say anything that can be interpreted as bad news.

Uncomfortable silences may occur during the listing stage of the critique. But the listing should not be done hastily. A speaker may be holding back a comment—especially if it is a positive one—that will come out only if extra time is allowed.

After the lists have been compiled, the tape should be run. The tape can be stopped at various points when one of the good features or one of the features that needs improvement appears (it doesn't have to be stopped at all of them, because some comments can be made while the tape is running). When the tape is stopped, the speaker should be encouraged to verbalize the criticism. The basic aim of the critique is to get the speaker involved in the evaluation with the long-range goal of having the speaker in the habit of monitoring the progress of a speech during delivery.

Viewing a tape of a speech can be a quite complex event for a speaker. The critique should not be rushed. It will be a good idea to turn the sound off at a point or two so the speaker may concentrate solely on physical behavior. Without the audio, the speaker's gestures, posture, and facial expression will stand out sharply.

When a speaker needs a great deal of improvement or when criticizing a speech of considerable importance, it may be wise to record more than one dress rehearsal performance. The additional practice may be recorded immediately while the needed changes are fresh on the speaker's mind, or it may be best to delay the next practice session to give the speaker time to reflect on the best way to deliver the speech. Circumstances will dictate the best approach.

HELPING THE SPEAKER WITH AUDIO-VISUALS

Part of the coaching function will be to give advice on the use of visual aids. This function actually begins with the first speaker-writer conference when the speech is being planned.

One fundamental principle should guide the speech writer: No audio-visual aid should be used as an end in itself. If an aid does not help present the idea more clearly than it can be presented without the aid or if it does not add a dimension of credibility or interest, then the aid is mere "eyewash" that will probably inhibit the interaction between speaker and audience.

Occasionally a speaker will want to use visual aids on the grounds that "everybody does it." Or the speaker may actually want the aid to serve as a distraction to keep audience attention away from the speaker's real or imagined weaknesses in speaking. Often speakers use visual aids out of habit; they haven't stopped to think about it for years.

After eliminating all the visual aids that aren't needed, the speech writer should consider pressing for fresh and interesting aids. Charts and slides need not be the only aids used. Speakers might be asked to confess their own reaction to the routine use of slides and charts in speeches they have to hear. Except for professional multi-media productions, most slide presentations are admittedly pretty dull.

Among the alternatives to charts and slides, consideration might be given to models and objects. An engineer speaking on the future of energy can increase interest by displaying a piece of oil shale or a jar of tar sand. An executive speaking on government regulation can bring out a stack of documents to demonstrate the paperwork required on a certain project. A speaker on the environment can show samples of water or particles removed from the air. When quoting from a report, a speaker might hold up the document.

Contrary to what many textbooks say, visual aids do not always have to be large enough to be seen in detail. Some aids are used for interest and credibility as demonstrated by the examples just cited.

In some cases a speaker should be encouraged to use a large pad, a chalkboard or an overhead projector to quickly sketch a diagram or to write key words or numbers. Material written during the presentation can enliven the speech if done properly. Only material that can be written quickly should be used; the speaker should keep talking by adding patter to fill the time or by memorizing or paraphrasing a section of the manuscript.

GUIDELINES FOR HANDLING AIDS

Don't Gaze at the Aid. Few sights are more ludicrous than an adult human being standing in front of an audience while engaged in earnest conversation with a chart on an easel. The speaker has the right to expect the correct picture will appear at the proper time, and a quick glance can tell the speaker if everything is in order. Beyond that, there can be little justification for the speaker to stare at the aid.

Keep Aids Simple. A visual aid displayed to clarify rather than to add credibility or interest must not be cluttered. Each aid should illustrate *one* idea with a clear point of focus. A somewhat complex aid can be shown by gradually building it up with overlays as the speaker guides the audience through the parts of the picture step by step.

Expose Only When Needed. The visual aid should be in view only at the point in a speech where it helps the audience understand the speaker's idea. An attractive visual brought up in advance will almost always deflect attention away from the speaker. Ideally, aids should be removed as soon as they are no longer needed, but audiences are usually not as likely to be distracted by an aid after it has been used as they are if it is presented before it is needed.

Make the Aid Visible. Except for aids that don't really need to be seen (in the case, for example, of a speaker who brandishes a silicone chip), care must be taken to make sure a listener's line of sight is not blocked by the lectern or by some object in the meeting room such as a support column. Pictures and charts must be big enough and must be drawn with heavy lines in bold colors. Any company audio-visual department will supply aids with these qualities and keep the speaker from having to ad-lib an embarrassed, "I know you can't see this clearly, but. . . ."

No Handouts During the Speech. Almost never will it be advisable to pass out material to an audience during a speech. Workshops and training sessions are exceptions, but the normal speech will suffer as members of an audience make their own use of the material. They tend to look at the wrong place when the speaker attempts to focus their attention, and they even find handouts suitable for doodling, making grocery lists, and con-structing paper airplanes. Especially distracting is the case where a single visual aid is handed out to be passed from listener to listener. If a handout must be distributed, it usually should be made available at the end of the speech.

Avoid Mindless Words, Phrases, and Symbols. Few people appreciate staring at the word "PRODUCTIVITY" while a speaker discourses on the subject. Nor do the cute figures of factory workers at their stations or secretaries typing offer the listener much help. The company logo on the screen for the initial two minutes of a speech does not promote corporate good will—such an opening should be left to MGM's lion and others in the entertainment field.

WORKING WITH THE AUDIO-VISUAL EXPERTS

Whether employing the services of an audio-visual depart-ment within an organization or buying A-V material from out-side, speech writers need to have a good working relationship with the technicians who supply these services. As in working with someone who furnishes information for speeches, the speech writer will find it useful to get to know the A-V experts before they are needed. The capacity of the department or the firm should be understood. Knowing the A-V capability will prevent both unreasonable expectations and under-use of available talent.

A-V technicians work, as speech writers do, under the pressure of deadlines. A writer needs to recognize that pressing demands from others who also need audio-visuals may affect the ability of an in-house department to respond. So, just as the writer should expect early notification of a writing assignment from a speaker, the technician should be told of A-V needs as soon as possible.

When dealing with anyone who is an expert in a technical field, a delicate balance must be struck. On the one hand, the writer should be open to suggestions and should take advantage of the expertise available. Excellent advice may be offered to improve the quality of the final product. On the other hand, a writer should not be too ready to accept the claim that "it can't be done." A request may be impossible to satisfy, but many times a way can be found if the writer presses the point and if the writer has built a good relationship with the A-V department.

PREPARING FOR THE QUESTION AND ANSWER SESSION

Based on his experience as a White House speech writer, William Safire reported on the preparation required for a president to face a Q&A session in the form of a press conference: "The fact is that a presidential press conference requires at least two days of hard homework. [The president's] staff will prepare about 75 questions, covering the approximately 25 that will be asked in a half hour and all those that go unasked. These, along with suggested answers, go into his 'black book' for review, occasional challenge and memorization. All presidents of the last two decades have done that homework." [*Richmond Times-Dispatch,* June 19, 1981]

Safire suggests the general direction to be followed by anyone who wishes to be well-prepared before facing a barrage of questions. Supplying a list of questions and answers is the first step.

In addition, the writer playing the role of speech coach may furnish tips on how the Q&A should be handled. Except in the most informal situations, the speaker will find it best to bring the speech to a formal conclusion and turn the program back over to the presiding officer to start the Q&A. This approach allows the speech itself to end on the climactic note the speech writer has included in the final paragraph of the manuscript. The speaker gets a round of applause, and the speaking segment of the program will be over.

If the speaker goes directly into the question and answer

session without bringing the speech to distinct conclusion, the transition is likely to be awkward. The rhythm of almost any Q&A session is slow at the beginning with a gradual increase in the tempo of responses from the audience as the session progresses. The speaker who remains at the lectern will be in a highly vulnerable spot if there is silence in reply to the offer to answer questions. Speakers at times will throw out "fillers" that prove to be embarrassing, as illustrated by the weakly stated, "Well, I guess I must have covered things pretty well. . . ."

It is far better for the speaker to have returned to a seat to allow the person in charge of the program to weather this potentially slow phase of the presentation. After someone is recognized to ask a question, the speaker can return to the stand and take over.

Remembering that the tempo of the Q&A tends to speed up, a speaker should be cautioned to take care in bringing the Q&A to an end. It may be that several hands will be in the air at once at the point time runs out. To avoid hurting feelings—and also to avoid looking as though the speaker is ducking questions—the speaker should announce a couple of minutes before time expires, "I see we have time for only a few more questions." If this is done, the speaker can safely cut the session off with hands still in the air. Even so it may be wise, if the speaker can spare the time, to agree to continue to respond to questions after the meeting has adjourned.

The Q&A session will go more smoothly if everyone in the audience realizes questions are to be allowed after the speech. The printed program and the presiding officer should both refer to this fact unless the audience has been fully conditioned to expect a question period following every talk.

TIPS ON HOW TO ANSWER QUESTIONS

Give Short Answers. A speaker may feel an urge to answer the easy questions at great length in order to be protected from the hard ones. While there is no way to dictate in advance the length of an answer, the rule to follow is "keep the answer as short as possible." If all answers are allowed to run as long as three minutes, the standard fifteen-minute question period would permit only five questions to be answered (compare this to the approximately one answer per minute Safire expects the president to answer). An occasional very short answer should be encouraged: "Yes, I fully agree," "No, we would not take that course if we had any other choice," or "Twelve percent last year." If a question is far too complicated to be answered, a speaker is entitled to suggest the direction of the answer in a sentence or two and offer to discuss the matter in private with the questioner. Short answers will be easier to give if the speaker can be trained to start with the heart of the answer rather than attempting to lead up to it.

Say "I Don't Know." If the speaker doesn't know the answer, a forthright "I don't know" is in order. It is usually wise to offer to find the answer and supply it to the person who asked the question. Few speakers have trouble realizing they don't know the answer to requests for specific data. The biggest danger comes when a broad question dealing with policy or opinion is asked and the speaker thinks the answer may occur while responding. All speakers need to be reminded that off-the-wall questions having nothing to do with the speech may be asked. At least some of these should get the "I don't know" response.

Repeating Questions. Far too many speakers fail to repeat questions asked too quietly for the audience to hear. Repeating is a courtesy the speaker should extend in large audiences. The speaker may benefit from the slight time allowed to think about the question. Also, questions can often be rephrased in language that is briefer and even somewhat more objective than that in which they were asked. The speaker should not, however, alter the basic meaning of a question.

Planting Questions. Speakers should never arrange to plant questions to take pressure off themselves. Questions of the "softie" sort are easily recognized by the audience and will hurt the speaker's credibility. Also, if a question is planted in a public meeting, the next day's headlines may include "Company Plants Stooge In Public Meeting." It may be useful to plant a question, however, if the object is to show that the speaker really intends to be open to whatever the audience wants to ask. A CEO who suspects an employee group will hold back on questions they really care about might have a couple of tough questions planted to get a session started.

Recognizing Questions. Once the question period gets under-way, the speaker should be in control. A person wishing to ask a question should be recognized directly and positively by the speaker. A speaker can point, call on people by location and/or sex and/or clothing, and can recognize questioners by name or position when known. Questioners should know when they have been called on.

Speakers should take care not to let a few people dominate a session. Some who want to ask questions will indicate their interest with a timid motion of the hand—speakers need to watch for such people. Special attention needs to be paid to the members of the audience sitting at the sides of the room or in the back. It will be best if no one asks a second question until everyone who wants to has had a chance to ask one question.

FACING HOSTILE QUESTIONS

However uncomfortable hostile questions may make a speaker feel, they do have two important benefits. First, they gain the speaker some sympathy. A speaker will seldom face an audience made up entirely of hostile listeners, but even in such a situation most people will appreciate the speaker's courage. When a hostile minority appears at a meeting, the neutral members of the audience will often express support for a speaker under attack.

Second, the venting process can alter the negative feelings of the hostile questioner. This does not apply to an implacable foe of the speaker, but a typical person who expresses anger in a question to a speaker will go away feeling better about the speaker and the speaker's organization.

Break Eye Contact with Hostile Questioners. When some-one asks a nasty question, the speaker should direct the answer, not to the person who asked it, but to the audience. If the speaker maintains eye contact with the questioner, that person might feel free to interrupt and start an unpleasant dialogue. When ending the answer to any question—especially a hostile one—the speaker should not return to the questioner and ask, "Did that answer your question?"

Keep Cool. The speaker can show determination in respond-ing to hostility but should not become angry. This is easier said than done, but practice in fielding hostile questions prepared by the speech writer can help. The dangers of not being prepared for hostility can be seen in a case in which a government official was being berated by questioners in a farm audience and in desperation blurted out, "You are lucky to be living in a country where you are free to ask questions like that!"

Only rarely will such a display of temper work to a speaker's advantage. Speakers should follow Kipling's advice to "keep your head when all about you are losing theirs and blaming it on you."

Don't Fall for Loaded Questions. If a hostile question contains loaded words, they have to be avoided in the answer or exposed to the audience as unfair. The answer to the question "Isn't it true that thermal pollution from your Rocky Creek plant has altered the ecology of Stone Lake?" may be yes. But the negative loading of "thermal pollution" and the negative loading of "altered the ecology" makes the correct answer sound negative. So, the speaker might find it advisable to violate the rule calling for immediately answering the question in a brief sentence or two, and instead the speaker would comment on the language of question. It might be suggested that the speaker wants the audience to understand that the terms used in the question refer to concepts that might be described in more objective language.

THE SPEECH WRITER AS ADVANCE AGENT

The speech writer, to protect the quality of the speech, may find it necessary to precede the speaker to a meeting place to check it out and then to be present to see that all goes well at the meeting. The role of an advance agent varies from speaker to speaker, and each agent needs to have an appropriate checklist to make sure the arrangements are in order.

The duties of an advance agent may run from carrying an extra copy of the manuscript to supplying the speaker with a slice of lemon before the speech. The advance agent will usually be seen in the meeting hall checking the microphone before the audience assembles. Minor changes in the text of the speech may be required if the speaking situation proves to be slightly different from that the writer was led to expect.

PREPARING FOR THE OVERSEAS SPEECH

Richard Charlton, speaking from his experience in helping a speaker prepare for foreign speeches, has sound advice to offer on translation difficulties:

> If a CEO ever needs an advance agent it's in an overseas speech environment. The speech writer or PR director should handle arrangements in advance of the speech to make sure it will achieve the desired goals.
>
> Use instant translation as little as possible. A speech always loses something in translation, and the more instantaneous, the more it loses.
>
> There are often better ways to communicate. For example, on one occasion the president of an American company which had just formed a partnership with a French firm, was invited to address 300 wary top management people in Paris. The president felt that his first task should be to give the French managers a comprehensive picture of the American company since they knew little about it.
>
> The speech writer convinced him he should create a good cassette slide presentation of the corporate story in French. A French A-V firm produced the presentation, with a well-known French TV commentator as narrator, based on an English text supplied by the writer. The presentation was followed by the president's speech, a thoughtful 10-minute talk on the future of the partnership delivered in English using a translator.
>
> The audience appreciated the fact the Americans had taken pains to present their corporate story in French with a familiar French voice. The president's earnest message at the conclusion was much better received than if the audience had first been made to endure 20 minutes of tedious translation of the U. S. company's history.
>
> The translation of the speech was not a truly instant sight-reading of the text or translation of words as they were spoken. That approach puts the translator under terrific pressure.
>
> Here are some suggestions to make translations effective:
>
> Deliver copies of the text of the speech to the translators the day before the speech. Be available to answer questions, explain jargon, spell out nuances.
>
> Have a news release translated and ready for distribution.
>
> Encourage translators to emphasize key points. If you've watched U.N. proceedings on TV, you know translators' words are often delivered with as much passion as a plumbing instructor.
>
> Hire only highly-skilled translators.
>
> Prevail on the speaker to deliver the address slowly, with frequent pauses. Have the speech typed in a format that indicates places to pause and encourages a slow pace.

Avoid visual aids if possible (as part of the actual speech).

Keep in mind that the English language is unique for its brevity. Five words in English may require eight or nine in French or Spanish.

Make sure microphones, lines to translators' booths, and headsets are working before the speech starts. There is a whole new dimension of opportunities for electronic malfunction. Be prepared.

CONCLUSION

The work of at least some speech writers does not end until the moment the speaker walks up to the lectern. Then the writer, like the caddy when the golfer hits the ball in a big tournament, can only hope the speaker is in good form.

Chapter IX

SPECIAL TYPES OF SPEECHES

"You will often have to perform appropriate acts of courtesy on public occasions—introduce a speaker, welcome a guest, present a gift or an award, etc. Custom requires you to say something." [William Norwood Brigance]

Not all speeches are major addresses dealing with burning issues. Many speeches of courtesy or ceremony must be written. Almost any corporation or other organization has its equivalent of the White House's "Rose Garden Rubbish." Former presidential speech writer John B. McDonald reviewed the 1972 *Public Papers of the Presidents* and counted, along with 432 major texts, 420 "Additional White House Releases," 346 "Additional White House Announcements," 78 "Proclamations," 55 "Executive Orders," 65 "Presidential Reports to Congress," and 15 other miscellaneous presidential documents. The president needed appropriate remarks for proclamations on National Beta Club Week, National Check Your Vehicle Emissions Month, and National Coaches Day. He also required remarks on the Great Lakes Basin Commission, the Swan Island Treaty, and the official position on procedures for use of off-road vehicles on public lands. [McDonald, p. A 11]

Special types of speeches have a number of characteristics that set them off from the standard public speech. They usually are short. They have a streamlined structure with little attention ordinarily paid to making major points or divisions of the talk emerge clearly; more attention is paid to subtle transitions. These speeches almost always have a friendly, social tone. They have little concern for the most part with proof or evidence. And they can be less conversational in language almost to the point of being "literary" in some instances.

The special types to be examined here are the speech of introduction, the speech of award or tribute, the dedication speech, the commencement address, and the speech to entertain.

156

THE SPEECH OF INTRODUCTION

The speech of introduction requires that three basic pieces of information be communicated to the audience: (1) the speaker's name, (2) the speaker's qualifications to talk on the topic, and (3) the title or subject matter of the speech. This information should be conveyed in less than three minutes with one to two minutes being a good range.

Most of the advice for constructing a good speech of introduction can best be phrased in the negative.

DON'T OVERDO IT

The speech of introduction should be low-key. In delivery and content, it should not be so dynamic that it becomes a hard act for the speaker to follow. Extravagant praise of the speaker should be avoided. Speeches of introduction should not promise an audience the speaker will be great. If the speaker *does* prove to be good, the audience can decide for itself. The introduction should merely serve to help make it clear to the audience that the speaker is *qualified* to speak. Even the humor should not be too good. If the introducer gets gales of laughter, the speaker's opening humor may appear weak by comparison.

DON'T USE CLICHES

Avoid such phrases as "A speaker who needs no introduction," "Without further ado," "It is a high privilege and a distinct honor," and "I am happy to present." Common sense substitutions can be used such as "Many of us have known our speaker during the ten years he has managed the Ajax plant in Centerville," "I know we are all interested in hearing what Bob has to say," and "I'm glad we were finally able to work out a time when our speaker could appear on one of our programs."

DON'T PREEMPT THE SPEAKER'S TOPIC

A speech of introduction that discusses the speaker's topic runs the risk of either taking away one of the speaker's ideas or, even worse, contradicting the speaker. References to the speaker's subject should be limited to its significance or timeliness.

Don't Include a False Ending

The good speech of introduction has a rhythm that builds to the point when the speaker stands and advances to the lectern with the applause of the audience welling up in greeting. If the speaker thinks the introduction has ended and starts to rise only to discover there is more to come, the experience can be unnerving. Although the speech of introduction may conclude with the speaker's topic, the safest way of ending finishes with the speaker's name: "Here, then, to give us a successful manager's perspective on that topic—Jane Jackson."

Don't Count on Inspiration

The speech of introduction should be written out in full and read without ad libs. Speaking from notes or memory in introducing a speaker can be a disaster. Introducers have been known to forget the name of the speaker. They often blurt out inane comments. And they can easily make errors in word choice of the sort that occurred when a presiding officer tried to thank a guest for filling in at the last minute by saying, "As most of you know, we weren't able to get the speaker we really wanted tonight. . . ."

Don't Read a Vita

Surprising as it may sound, a simple autobiographical data sheet can become a dangerous tool in the hands of some program organizers. They will read an entire three-page vita of a speaker or they will select arbitrary, ill-chosen segments for an introduction. A good rule, then, calls for the speech writer to prepare a speech of introduction for the use of the person who has the responsibility of introducing the speaker. This speech can usually be written double spaced on a single page *in vita form.* To avoid possible offense, it should not be identified as a speech of introduction, but can be labeled, "Background information on Mr. Jones for his address to the Town Club on January 12."

The introduction writers prepare for their own speakers to deliver in introducing other speakers may be somewhat more elaborate than the bare-bones type limited to a single page. The longer introduction allows for personal comments on the qualification of the speaker, for example, although these comments should not extend to promising that the speech will be good. This style of introduction can be somewhat more elevated in language than the other.

Here is a sample taken from the last paragraph of an introduction written in the "vita style" followed by a sample of the "personal" style:

> Mr. Price joined Wellhead Oil in 1970 as Director of Corporate Writing. He has supervised the departments of internal and external communication and was responsible for the creation of the award winning employee magazine, *Gush*. Mr. Price's topic for discussion in his appearance in Midtown is "Speaking Up and Speaking Out."

> For more than ten years Tom Price has directed a dynamic communication program at Wellhead Oil. He has helped make Wellhead an industry leader in addressing public issues. And Tom has recognized the crucial role of internal communications. He created Wellhead's employee publication, *Gush*, which in the past eight years has won three Silver Key awards—quite a record! To address us on the topic "Speaking Up and Speaking Out," we could not have found a better qualified communicator than . . . . Mr. Thomas V. Price.

THE SPEECH OF AWARD OR TRIBUTE

Service awards, retirements, speaker bureau activity citations, prize-winning suggestions—these and many more occasions require a speech of tribute. Such a speech can be built upon three principles: (1) pour on the praise, (2) back it up with a concrete example, and (3) include a personal note from the speaker.

The praise in an award situation can hardly be too heavy. If an employee is being rewarded for saving a thousand dollars with a suggestion on the assembly line, that thousand dollars can be multiplied by the number of employees in the company to show how much the contribution of an individual can mean. Whatever courage, brains, effort, or endurance has been demonstrated should be extolled in the warmest terms.

The accomplishment of the individual must be made concrete. The speech can not possibly fit any other individual. If a prize-winning suggestion was made by someone on the job for only a year, that can be the hook on which to hang the talk. Or if the speaker bureau member had to drive through a snow storm to give a talk in order to become eligible for an award, that can be mentioned.

The speaker must make the presentation personal. If the speaker has no way at all of knowing the person, then at least arrange for information to get to the speaker from a supervisor so the speaker can say, "In discussing the person we honor here today, the plant manager told me. . . ."

HUMOR IN THE AWARD SPEECH

The retirement speech generally has a touch of humor, as do some of the other award speeches. In such situations, humor serves to take the edge off the embarrassment that the speaker or the award recipient might feel. Humor should not be considered mandatory, however. Unless both speaker and recipient are comfortable with it, it will not work. Friendliness and warmth will accomplish the required ends as well as humor does.

THE DEDICATION SPEECH

As Professor William Norwood Brigance has observed, "We cannot complete any public building or monument only with stone and mortar. It is never completed until the speeches are made." [Brigance p. 490] Brigance goes on to suggest several themes that can be used in the dedication speech.

First, from both a practical and a symbolic point of view, the use of a new plant or a new project can be discussed. Second, the individuals who planned and constructed the plant or project can be praised. And, third, the future impact of the new facility can be explored.

THE COMMENCEMENT SPEECH

A commencement speech can be a slightly altered version of the ordinary public speech discussed in earlier chapters. A speaker representing a particular industry, for example, might simply make a speech on the future of the country from the perspective of that industry. With a few topical references to the occasion, the speech would meet the demands of the situation.

Many commencement speeches are much more ceremonial in

nature. They address broad and abstract themes. For better or worse, most of them are promptly forgotten if they are listened to at all.

The speaker's job, then, is to present a talk that does not violate the spirit of the occasion. The topic should almost never be controversial—graduates feel a great sense of release from authority on commencement day and are prone to express themselves rudely if they find they have to endure an extra lecture.

The spirit of the occasion will be violated by a long speech. Fifteen minutes marks the outer limits, but too much under ten minutes of speaking may not appear to do justice to the invitation. Rarely will a commencement speaker find it advisable to refer to the length of the speech. A promise to keep the remarks short may draw applause and will tend to denigrate the speaker's effort. A pithy twelve minutes will be appreciated without any effort on the part of the speaker to brag on the brevity of the address.

The essentials of the commencement address may be characterized somewhat casually as (1) NOTE, (2) GLOAT, (3) QUOTE, and (4) FLOAT.

First, the speech must take NOTE of all the people involved in the occasion. No matter how repetitious it may sound to someone who attends graduations frequently, the parents of the graduates should be credited for their contribution to the successful completion of schooling. So should the administration of the school and the faculty. A kind word for alumni and donors would not be out of order. And, of course, the graduating class must be recognized for its accomplishment.

Second, hyperbole has its place in a commencement address. The speaker should GLOAT in the sense of the term that means to gaze with admiration and affection. The honor of the invitation to speak can be mentioned even though such invitations are at times not too subtle hints for a contribution to the school or an effort to borrow the speaker's prestige for a school that needs its reputation polished. The school itself should be praised for whatever accomplishments the writer can dig up. The city, the state, the founders, the library, the athletic program, or anything else that has any worth at all can be subjects for praise.

Third, the speech can have a faint scholarly or literary ring. A QUOTE or two of suitable merit can be included by a speaker who in other situations might not be inclined to use such material. The text of the speech itself can be a bit more literary than usual. More attention can be paid to alliteration, to balance, to rhythm, to climax, to rhetorical questions than would be the case if the speaker were addressing a civic club at a noon meeting.

Fourth, the speech can FLOAT a vision of the future. This standard theme of the commencement address requires the speaker to assert that the future is bright or challenging or dangerous or wonderful. The speech might contain a few helpful suggestions on getting the most from the future or avoiding its pitfalls. The speaker's experience and reputation can be cited here to bolster modest suggestions for success.

THE HUMOROUS COMMENCEMENT ADDRESS

In recent years students who have had a voice in selecting commencement speakers have shown a preference for celebrities and for entertaining speeches. A humorous speech of the sort that Art Buchwald might give would be well received, but humor of that quality is both hard to produce and hard to deliver. If a speaker has a flair for light material, however, this possibility should not be overlooked.

THE SPEECH TO ENTERTAIN

Only rarely are speakers called on to give purely entertaining speeches. The principal types of speeches in which humor is the end and not a means are the after-dinner speech and the presentation at a roast.

THE ROAST

The roast speech is perhaps the most difficult of the two. The fine art of the humorous insult requires a deft touch. The essence of the roast gibe is that it must be broad enough to be unreal and true enough to fit the character of the person who is the butt of the humor. The subject matter of the jokes should be something that in some way can be seen as a virtue. Even Dean

Martin's drinking, apart from its value in giving Mr. Martin a ready means of audience identification, has its positive aspects because of the implied compliment in the "what a great drinker he is" message.

All of these characteristics are seen in a joke President Reagan made at a dinner honoring Bob Hope. It was not true, Mr. Reagan claimed, that Hope entertained the troops at Yorktown—he was at Valley Forge. The gibe fits Bob Hope as a dedicated USO entertainer and it teases him about his age (read "durability") as an implicit virtue.

On the other hand, when President Carter in a different roast situation said that Governor Jerry Brown was California's way of celebrating the International Year of The Child, the humor was not well received. The exaggeration was not broad enough to fall outside the range of what Mr. Carter might have said in earnest; the bite of the joke was too sharp.

THE AFTER-DINNER SPEECH

Some speeches after dinner are not intended to be funny. They may use a small amount of humor, but they are simply regular speeches that happen to be given after a meal. The speech under consideration here, the humorous after-dinner speech, is one which has entertainment as its major objective. The after-dinner speech does have a message; if it did not then the presentation would no longer be a speech but a comedy routine. The message, however, remains subordinate to the humor.

The message can be tacked on at the end of the speech—a fairly common practice with after-dinner speeches having an inspirational theme—or it can be the theme of the speech is loosely supported by the humor.

Apart from deciding where the message will appear, the after-dinner speech has little structure other than a string of humorous bits. The tried and true pieces of humor should be spread out somewhat to assure that all the laughter doesn't come in one short segment of the speech, but the pattern of organization can be highly flexible.

Here are some examples. A speech on the topic of consumer service presented at an awards banquet for a group of utility employees might consist of a series of stories about problems with consumers. Anecdotes can be cited and excerpts from letters read. The speech can be padded with material on consumers and human relations gathered from standard sources of humor in the public library. The speech can end with a few comments on the difficulty of working with customers and the importance of seeing the lighter side of the job.

An inspirational humorous speech can be developed on the subject of sales. Anecdotes, one-liners, and quotes on selling can lead to a brief motivational passage on the importance of sales and the sales force. The shift from the humorous to the inspirational is possible because the humor creates an emotional response in the audience and the conclusion of the speech keeps the emotional pitch high, but redirects it to a new channel.

No speech writer should be expected to have the ability to write humor at the level of a professional comedy writer. For very important speeches, then, it may well be wise to invest in the services of a specialist. Writing a successful joke is a difficult task, one at which few writers have had the opportunity to gain experience.

CONCLUSION

From Lincoln's Gettysburg Address to the most recent inaugural speech by a U.S. president, the ceremonial speech has played a significant role in the history of speech making. Even more than most speeches, these special types of addresses must fit the circumstances in which they are given. More important than their content is their style and their tone. Lincoln's suggestion at Gettysburg that "the world will little note nor long remember what we say here" was not true for the spirit of his speech. It would have been accurate for the substance of his address had he not sounded the right note of appropriate eloquence. His observation was fully accurate for the excellent oration by Edward Everett which preceded Lincoln's speech. Most people don't even remember the name of the other speaker at Gettysburg—the one who spoke for two hours.

CHAPTER X

THE SPEECH IN THE COMMUNICATIONS PROGRAM

"Finally—and perhaps most importantly—the chief executive in the year 2000 will have a personal responsibility for advocacy, activism and outspokenness. Increasingly, the CEO will be expected to represent articulately and coherently his company and industry to their critics."
[David Rockefeller, *Vital Speeches,* January 1, 1980]

For centuries the demise of public speaking as a significant form of communication has been predicted. Plato believed philosophy with its logical and methodical search for ultimate truth would eliminate the need for speeches. When the printing press came along, it seemed no longer necessary to gather audiences for a message that could be printed in mass quantities and distributed to be read at leisure. Then radio . . . . Then television. . . .

But public speaking endures. It remains a simple and effective means of communication. And it has become, in the Western world at least, part of our social fabric. What politician would dare run for office only on the strength of skillfully produced commercials and ads? What minister would be content to trust in sensitivity groups to replace the message from the pulpit?

Business speaking, a product of the twentieth century, shows steady growth. The increase in corporate speaking occurs at the same time companies are making excellent use of media unheard of a few decades ago. Closed circuit television supplements the old-fashioned bulletin board. Employee publications have the professional touch of the best national news magazines. Multimedia presentations rival the dramatic power of the movie screen. The parallel growth of speaking with the newer media of communication can be found, not only in corporations, but in non-profit organizations, in government agencies, and in the professions as well.

165

A STRATEGY FOR SPEAKING

Partly as a result of the assumption that speeches are delivered "on demand," an organization may not have a conscious strategy for using speech as a medium of communication. It is not necessary to wait for invitations to speak or for occasions where a speech is required by circumstances. Invitations may be solicited by subtle or direct means. Employees may be asked to generate requests for speeches from groups they belong to. Direct approaches may be made to officers in charge of programs; any company officer who serves on the directing body of a community organization with the president of a university has the chance to make known a willingness to speak to students. Brochures may be mailed making the availability of speakers known.

Any successful organization with a marketing program knows its market. But all too often, a corporation with a desperate need to communicate does not have a clear notion of target audiences for speeches.

A list of desired audiences could be drawn up. It might give attention to hostile groups or disinterested audiences the company needs to reach. A clear policy should be stated in regard to school groups. Are major efforts in responding to elementary schools requests for speakers in the company's best interest or is the company merely making the day easier for teachers? Does the company need to reach college groups? If so, should the message be aimed at business students or at liberal arts classes or at some other segment of the population?

Maybe too many speeches are being given to audiences that don't need the message. If a company has almost all its speaking effort devoted to "damn the government" talks before civic club audiences that already agree with the idea, then the value of such speeches might be questioned.

The prestige of audiences must be considered. One talk to a group of opinion leaders may be worth dozens of speeches to lesser groups. Some audiences give the speaker a hearing beyond the confines of company or community. If an organization has a speaker who aspires to be viewed as an industry leader, speeches will be one avenue to that goal.

A balance should be planned among employee, public, and industry/professional audiences. The division need not be even, but it should represent the organization's communication needs and not some chance or arbitrary expenditure of time and energy.

A frank assessment should be made of the abilities of available speakers. Their strong points and weak points should be considered in planning the best way to use each person. Care must be taken not to overburden good speakers or the top officials in an organization. Almost routinely, requests for speakers will be for the highest ranking person in the field, but acceding to such requests may not always be the best course of action. A "tier" system might be considered with one set of objectives for the highest ranking officers and another for a level of speakers taken from middle management.

The considerations cited here do not exhaust the possible concerns that should enter into the planning of a speech communication strategy. They do, however, suggest some of the reasons communication through speeches should not be left to chance.

THE SPEAKERS BUREAU

A speakers bureau offers an excellent way to harness the speaking power of an organization. A bureau can reach a surprising number of people. Of, for example, an organization had 50 speakers giving two speeches a month, they would reach 1200 audiences in a year. With an average of only 40 people in an audience, 48,000 listeners would get the message or messages the bureau wanted to deliver. And each message could be tailored to fit the needs of the particular segment of the mass audience being addressed.

BUREAU SUPPORT

For a speakers bureau to work, it must have top management support. The outlay required in time, energy, and money is simply too great to sustain without backing from management in the form of budget and prestige.

A speakers bureau cannot be grafted onto a full-blown communications program. It demands more than a few extra hours a month from a secretary and a director. Unless some other program is being phased out or downgraded, additional personnel will be needed to run a bureau properly. Speaker bureaus have a habit of succeeding better than expected. Legitimate requests for speakers may soon tax the ability of the bureau to train speakers, process invitations to speak, and keep the extensive records a well-managed bureau should have. There must be an adequate budget to sustain this level of activity.

The prestige factor may determine whether a bureau begins its life in a healthy state. With a few encouraging words from the powers that be, the better candidates for the bureau are likely to emerge. Also, the supervisors of the speakers will be more cooperative if the bureau has warm approval at the highest levels. Supervisors can have a negative influence on the desire of speakers to volunteer. A few cool remarks from a boss can dampen the ardor of a speaker who otherwise might be an active member of the bureau.

OBJECTIVES

A speakers bureau should have clear goals, goals consistent with the overall objective of an organization's total speaking program. Bureaus that have been in existence for a number of years may lose sight of their reason for being. At least once a year a bureau director should restate and reassess bureau aims.

In spite of the danger of wandering away from its original path, a bureau's flexibility can be a virtue. If communication goals change, the bureau can change. If a problem arises suddenly and needs to be addressed, the bureau can be the medium to accomplish the task.

A brief review of the basic ends of a single speech—to inform, to stir feelings, to change belief, and to get action—can provide a framework for analysis of the objectives of an entire bureau. Like any one speech, a bureau must be designed to bring about change in listeners.

THE DIRECTOR

A good speakers bureau director will be a benevolent dictator. The director must be benevolent because the bureau is run not for the director but for the larger aims of the organization and because the bureau depends on volunteers who give their services out of a sense of conviction and duty. The director must be a sort of dictator because a bureau can get out of hand if not properly managed.

A director needs to pay particular attention to the assignment of speakers. As has already been noted, the right speaker should be assigned to each speech to make sure speaking resources are employed to best advantage. The director should also make sure that the better speakers are not overworked. No bureau member should be authorized to accept an invitation to represent the organization. All invitations should be forwarded to the director who then decides who speaks to whom.

Pattern Speeches. The bureau director should have the responsibility for seeing that each speaker is supplied with an official pattern talk for each speech on the bureau's list. While most speakers should speak from notes and all speakers should adapt each talk to fit the needs of the speaking situation, the pattern talk remains a valuable speaker aid. It should serve as a model of organization, and it can guide a speaker in choosing language to express ideas.

The pattern talk also serves as a guide to organizational policy. Speakers need to be aware of any area where they might create confusion by speaking carelessly on policy, and in such an area they should follow the pattern talk closely.

Because pattern talks can rapidly get out of date, the bureau director should supply supplementary material on a regular basis. One common practice is to give each member of the bureau all the pattern talks in a binder. New data can then be mailed to everyone with instructions for the fresh information to be filed in the binder with the appropriate speech. Speakers should be encouraged to save and share relevant information they discover on their own.

Pattern talks will, of course, have to be rewritten periodically, and sometimes a speech outlives its usefulness to the point that it has to be pulled from the program.

Visual and Audio Aids. Speakers can be expected to supply only some of their audio and visual aids. Furnishing aids to speakers must be taken into account when planning the budget and staff of a bureau. Some aids must be available in multiple sets to make it possible for two or more speeches in large bureaus to be given simultaneously and to accommodate speakers who travel long distances from headquarters and therefore might not be able to return material for several days.

Providing most of the visual aids gives the bureau director another control mechanism to make sure both the quality and content of the aids meet the organization's standards. Any charts and slides should have a professional look to avoid making speakers appear amateurish in their presentations.

Audience Analysis. While speakers should be urged to conduct their own individual audience analysis, the director has the responsibility of seeing that the job is accomplished. It may be wise for the director to supply initial basic data on the audience such as size, age range, sex makeup, and other basic demographic information. The director should also supply forms which suggest other details the speakers must attempt to uncover such as level of audience knowledge and listener attitude toward the topic of the speech. The material explained in Chapter III will be useful in constructing a guide to proper audience analysis.

Feedback. A speaker bureau director should be forthright in the effort to collect feedback from audiences. Speakers should aid in this effort, but at least part of the feedback, that which evaluates the effectiveness of the speakers, should go directly to the bureau director.

The speaker should be provided with a feedback form for each speech and should be instructed to fill it out as soon as possible after the speech. Where possible the feedback should be recorded on the same day the speech is delivered. The speaker should be asked to give a report on the response of the audience during the speech to attempt to gauge the degree of interest in the subject and the extent to which the speaker was successful in informing, stimulating, convincing, or actuating the group. The form should include space for the speaker to list in detail the questions the listeners asked in the Q&A. Any other useful information gathered in conversations before or after the speech should also be recorded. The speaker should supply an accurate count of the number of people who attended the speech along with any notations about persons of special importance who were present.

A speaker evaluation form filled out by selected members of

an audience can be used in a variety of ways. For some speeches a spot check is all that is required, and a single evaluation form may be supplied to the person in charge of the program. For other speakers and speeches the director may decide that a larger sample should be used, and the organization can be asked to have all the officers or even all the members fill out the form. Most audiences will cooperate in this effort, but obviously there could be some groups where discretion would dictate that no request for evaluation be made.

The evaluation form can request information on delivery of the speech or on its impact on the audience, or both types of information can be requested.

A simple check list on delivery might ask that the speaker be rated on a scale of perhaps 1 to 5 (excellent to adequate) on such items as physical behavior and voice, clarity of organization, effectiveness of language, and impressiveness of content.

Also, a rough scale can be constructed to get an approximate idea of how the speech affected the audience. For example, the form might ask, "How do you feel about the ideas advanced in the speech: Strongly Agree—Mildly Agree—Neutral—Mildy Disagree—Strongly Disagree," "Did this speach cause you to change your attitude toward the [speaker's organization]: very positive change—slight positive change—no change—slight negative change —very negative change," or "Following the speech did you feel you understood [the organization's] position: a lot better—a little better—the same—less well—much less well."

A Speaker's Kit. Some of the material discussed above can be provided to the speakers in a folder the speakers should keep on file. The pattern speeches and the up-dated material should go in this "speaker's kit." It should also include the audience analysis forms and samples of forms used to evaluate the speaker. It might be expanded to include a list of tips on delivery and suggestions on handling the Q&A.

Publicity. The bureau and its speeches should be advertised. Where appropriate, press coverage should be sought for speeches. This may be especially beneficial in smaller towns or rural areas. The bureau itself must be publicized at least in its initial stages. In addition to soliciting help from employees in making the bureau known, the director should attempt to draw up a list of current officers or other contacts in target groups to construct a mailing list for speaker bureau brochures. In some cases a display set up in lobbies or other public places can advertise the bureau.

Record Keeping. Bureau directors should maintain a log of bureau activities. The log should make it easy for the director to prepare a detailed quarterly or annual report indicating the number of audiences the bureau reached and the total number of listeners who heard the speeches. This information may be especially useful if it breaks the audiences down by types and relates the types of audiences to the various messages the speakers are presenting.

Such a record enables the director to tell at a glance which speakers are overworked and which ones need to be exhorted to do more. It also suggests the level of demand for the bureau to guide the director in recruiting new speakers.

All press releases, evaluation forms, and letters of appreciation should be retained to help provide a basis for justification of the bureau's existence.

REINFORCING SPEAKERS

Only rarely are speaker bureau members paid for their efforts, and in some cases they are not even fully reimbursed for all their expenses. But even when speakers do get money for speaking the amounts are usually modest and cannot be expected to supply adequate motivation for spending the time and effort it takes to make speeches. Most bureaus find it advisable to offer additional incentive.

Awards. From lapel pins to certificates to gold watches, speaker bureau directors find ways to reward speakers. In some cases everyone gets the same recognition for membership in the bureau. In others the awards may offer varying degrees of recognition based on length of service or number of speeches. Sometimes a letter of commendation from the chief executive officer of the organization can supplement the award system.

Newsletters. A regular form of communication from the bureau director to the speakers can be one means of reinforcement. A speakers bureau newsletter can also serve to encourage speakers by reporting what other members of the bureau are doing. A newsletter may include useful tips—sometimes supplied by bureau members. It can report the kinds of questions audiences are asking, it can carry news on fresh information being supplied for the speeches, and it can even contain humor to keep spirits up.

Banquets. An annual or semiannual luncheon or dinner meeting may be an excellent way to reinforce speakers in their work. A personal word of encouragement from top management can be easily delivered in such a setting and a speaker can be brought in to address some of the issues considered in the bureau speeches. The banquet obviously offers an ideal opportunity for award presentations to speakers.

THE PROFESSIONAL SPEAKER

Sometimes an organization's message can best be delivered by a speaker who is paid to do the job on either a full- or part-time basis. Celebrities are sometimes hired for this purpose—an actor or an athlete who is widely known can become a popular speaker. In some cases experts from the academic world, especially in the areas of economics or science, have a slight edge over a regular employee. Of course, an employee could be hired for the purpose of making speeches or employees with considerable speaking ability or special areas of expertise could be assigned as full-time speakers for a specified period.

The "hired gun" approach to speech making has one major disadvantage. The hired speaker does not have the extra boost in credibility that comes from a person who can say, "I'm doing this over and above my regular duties because I think it's important for you to get this message."

TRAINING MEMBERS OF A SPEAKERS BUREAU

A speakers bureau should attract persons with better-than-average speaking skills. Even so, training is almost always a good idea.

For one thing, some bureau members may have learned to speak in one of the "how to be confident in front of an audience" schools. As a result, they may be making serious mistakes in a highly confident manner. But even the good speakers should benefit from a review of speech techniques. In addition, a training session helps build *esprit de corps* among bureau members. And such training gives the director a chance to see the speakers in action, to assess the ways in which each speaker can best be used, and to determine if some speakers should quietly be eliminated from the program.

A training program also permits a reasonable degree of control over policy. The individual changes speakers make in the pattern talks can be monitored to make certain no major errors are committed. Since more than one speaker may be speaking on the same topic in training, speakers get a chance to see the subject from a perspective other than their own.

Speakers also benefit by having the opportunity for a dry run before they face an outside audience. Even experienced speakers will appreciate the practice as an opportunity to try out a new talk or experiment with changes in one they have given before.

The ideal training session will be limited to speaker bureau members and will be designed to get them ready to deliver a bureau speech. This type of training focuses on the needs of the bureau in a way that will not be possible in training from Toastmasters, a college night class, or a professional speech training firm with a fixed program. The alternatives are better than no training at all, but they should not be the speaker bureau director's preferred solution.

In-house trainers can be used if qualified staff members are available. This approach will be the best for policy control and will probably be the least expensive type of training.

If an outside trainer is used, here are some guidelines to follow in setting up the program:

(1) Insist on training that includes both theory and practice. Either extreme should be avoided. If a trainer does nothing more than listen to speeches and evaluate them, the speakers will gain little in the way of principles they can apply to other speeches. On the other hand, a series of lectures on the techniques of speaking will be of relatively little value if they are not put into practice and critiqued.

(2) Insist that the trainer know the objectives of the bureau and that the trainer support these objectives. Any trainer who does not insist on seeing pattern speeches in advance and who does not make

careful inquiries about the nature of the speaking program should be suspect from the start. Any trainer who is condescending in attitude should not be hired.

(3) Insist that the trainer supply references. References should be studied, and they should be checked out by conversation with previous employers.

(4) Insist on monitoring the training. The training should be observed by the director or the director's representative at least the first few times a trainer is used. Often it is a good idea to have sessions open to higher management so the progress of the training can be seen firsthand. A training session should serve both to build speaking skills and to prepare communications staff personnel to either conduct the training themselves or to at least be better prepared to observe and evaluate speakers in the field.

(5) Insist on program evaluation. Have each speaker fill out a critique of the training with special emphasis on finding out how the training affected the speaker's performance.

(6) Insist on relevant content. Some speech trainers still spend too much time on such relatively unimportant areas as voice quality and standard pronunciation. Do not employ an out-of-work elocutionist to train a modern speaker.

If a director must choose between training a large number of speakers in a shallow program or training a smaller number in a thorough program, the second alternative should be selected. A director will usually be better off with a few well-trained speakers than with greater numbers of speakers inadequately prepared for their job.

A MODEL PROGRAM

A training model that has been used successfully many times involves 10 to 12 participants in three days of lecture/discussions and exercises. The material covered in the lecture/discussions includes speech delivery, audience analysis, speech objectives, patterns of organization, using evidence to support ideas, oral language and semantics, handling the Q&A, and persuasion.

One-half of the time is used for explanation of these topics and discussion of their application. The other half is devoted to four speaking exercises. The exercises consist of a warm-up talk (3-5 minutes), a model miniature speech (5-7 minutes), a speech introducing another participant's speech (1-3 minutes), and a dress rehearsal of a bureau speech (15-20 minutes). All speeches are recorded on video tape and played back for evaluation. The last speech is opened to questions by the participants who play the role of the audience designated by the speaker. That speech and its critique require the entire third day of the program.

FOLLOW-UP TRAINING

After a speaker has been a member of a bureau for two or three years, follow-up training will usually be advisable. Less time might be devoted to formal lecture or discussion in this training with more emphasis spent on critique of performance. A speaker might, for example, be asked to repeat a recent speech which would be taped and evaluated.

This type of training can be done in small groups or it can be conducted on a one-to-one basis. In some instances it can be accomplished by having a staff member sit in on an actual speech and build the training around observations of the speaker's performance.

Follow-up training polishes skills, it reinforces speakers by reminding them that the organizations still cares about their performance, and it serves to check on any possible deviations from policy that may have crept into speeches.

MORE SOPHISTICATED MEASUREMENT OF SPEECH RESULTS

In the case of either a major speech by an executive or an occasional speakers bureau talk, it may be useful to measure the change in an audience more precisely than would be possible with any method discussed so far. The services of a professional polling agency would be required for such a measurement.

Increasingly, communicators responsible for speaking programs may discover that demands for greater "productivity" apply to their work. The mere counting of the number of speeches, speakers, audiences, and topics covered may not provide adequate proof of a program's success.

Some speech writers have the mistaken notion that the effect of speeches cannot be accurately determined. That is not the case. The effect of a speech *can* be measured, but the effort—and the cost—will be considerable.

The greater problem, one which was discussed earlier in this chapter, is that of deciding in advance what the speech communication program should accomplish. If the program aims to change attitudes, then attitudes can be measured before and after the speech to determine the extent of the change. If the program aims to raise the level of information, then the increase in what an audience knows after a speech, if any, can be tested.

A professional polling organization could, for example, telephone a representative sample of the membership of a major civic group prior to a speech and establish the level of opinion or information at that time. Follow-up polls checking with people who heard the speech could establish the change with a specified degree of accuracy.

PRESS COVERAGE OF SPEECHES

In some instances, as in a major political address, a speaker may aim for an audience far broader than the listeners present at the speech. Such a speech reaches and affects its prime audience through the news media. Even in the case of those speeches where the most important audience is the one physically present, additional press coverage may be valuable.

Given the small amount of space or time likely to be afforded a typical speech by the media, it is realistic to expect that little of the substance of a talk will be reported. Indeed, because of the need of most reporters for a "lead," a news story may often appear distorted from the speech writer's perspective. Except in rare instances, speech writers should expect the speaking event to get more coverage than the material in the speech.

This kind of publicity can still be useful. It advertises the speaking program, it may get a little of the message over, and it will probably be a boost to the ego of the speaker.

Important speeches usually deserve a press release. And, while opinions differ on this matter, providing the press with an advance copy of the speech will often be a good idea.

WHAT HAPPENS TO THE SPEECH AFTER DELIVERY

In the spring of 1974 the head of Exxon gave a speech at Rutgers University in which he spoke forcefully on the preservation of private enterprise. The public affairs department decided to print 100,000 copies of the speech for distribution to people it had targeted as a good secondary audience for the speech. The copies were mailed with a "hang-on" signed by the vice president for public affairs.

The mailing elicited 773 letters with requests for 38,000 additional copies. Fifteen requests for the right to reprint the speech were received from publications with a total circulation of 700,000. The letters came from a great variety of sources including 100 college professors, 20 other oil companies, and 14 Chambers of Commerce. Only 72 of the 773 letters were unfavorable.

Economist John Kenneth Galbraith was on the original target audience list, and he wrote a review attacking the speech in *The New York Times Book Review*. As a result, Exxon received another wave of requests for copies, many of them from people who felt that if Galbraith disliked the speech it must be good. A negative notice of the speech also appeared in Milton Moskowitz's nationally syndicated column. It too resulted in a number of requests for reprints.

Exxon finally printed 150,000 copies of the address. Although the Rutgers speech response was not at all typical of the reaction to the six to eight speeches Exxon annually reprinted at that time, the coordinator of creative services in the public affairs department, Otto W. Glade, summarized his feelings on the reprinting of speeches by saying, "It's additional mileage and for us it has been a worthwhile venture." [Glade, pp. 20-22]

THE TARGET AUDIENCE

Keeping an up-to-date mailing list for reprinted speeches can be a problem and the costs can be considerable. But in at least some cases the reprint can be added with little extra expense to mail already going to such groups as stockholders or employees. Special attention should be paid to mailing reprints to sources likely to reprint it. These include distant newspapers that would not have covered the speech, political figures who might quote the speech or include it in the *Congressional Record*, and the editor of *Vital Speeches*.

A few special comments on *Vital Speeches* may be in order. This twice-a-month publication with ten to twelve speeches per issue is the most widely read compilation of speeches in North

America. It is found routinely in all major libraries. *Vital Speeches* seeks to print speeches as they were delivered (it carried President Carter's slip of the tongue in his Democratic National Convention speech in 1980 as "Hubert Horatio Hornblower Humphrey"). The editor therefore does not usually alter copy, and a typographical error in a speech manuscript will be printed as is.

Because the *Vital Speeches* format includes a title and a subtitle, a brief digression on titles of speeches may be in order. Traditionally, speeches, unlike written communications, have not had titles. Titles are afterthoughts. No one knew at the time that Lincoln was delivering "The Gettysburg Address" or that Patrick Henry was giving a speech to be called "Give Me Liberty or Give Me Death." But titles are necessary for publication and occasionally are required for printed programs in advance of a meeting. A title should serve two functions. It should attract attention and it should concisely express the subject of the talk. The title plus sub-title makes it easy for a writer to accomplish both objectives.

It would be unfair to say that *Vital Speeches* ignores the quality of speeches, but the failure of the editor to print a speech submitted should not be taken by the writer as a mark of failure. The publication will carry most major political speeches, and if the number of speeches available is great some good speeches will not be published. *Vital Speeches* favors current material and is unlikely to use a speech after several months have passed.

FORMAT

The standard format for printed speeches seems to be the 3½ x 8½ inch pamphlet designed to fit in a regular business envelope. Only a few variations on this format are seen. Perhaps because organizations do not wish to appear to be spending a lot of money on reprints, many of them are rather dull and unattractive in appearance. Some efforts to enliven reprints include adding a picture of the speaker, highlighting quotations from the speech on the inside cover, attaching a few samples of the Q&A at the end, using a little artwork on the cover. More effort could be paid to this matter.

The "hang on" used by Exxon is basically a special type of

business card included with the talk to indicate who sent it. An address printed on the pamphlet is, of course, a good idea since it won't get lost and will aid anyone who wants to write for more reprints.

OTHER USES OF A SPEECH AFTER DELIVERY

Smaller radio stations often are able to use taped excerpts from speeches. A video tape of a speech can be made to show to employees or other interested groups. A small number of audio or video tapes may be mailed in place of printed speeches. This will not be a frequent practice, but some tapes of this sort do circulate because of such factors as the speaker's outstanding delivery, the use of especially interesting visual aids, or the presence of certain types of humor that are better heard than read.

However weary a writer may be after a speech has finally been written, the idea of doing something more with it should be given careful consideration. All that work should not always end up in a file drawer.

CONCLUSION

Although we live in a highly sophisticated communication environment, old-fashioned public speaking still has impact. It deserves to be treated as one of the major weapons in the communication arsenal of any organization with a message to deliver. A live speaker before a live audience remains a vital force, and the record of the encounter between the two, in print or on tape, may extend the influence of the speech even more.

BIBLIOGRAPHY

Alexander, Judd H. "Solid Waste Disposal Charges" (*Vital Speeches of the Day*, February 1, 1979).

Anderson, W. S. "Keynote Address," A speech before the Conference on Technology Transfer, Washington, D.C., December 7, 1977, by the Chairman of NCR Corporation.

Auer, J. Jeffrey. "Who Writes Parliamentary Speeches? Political Speechwriting in England" (A paper read at the Annual Convention of the Central States Speech Association, Chicago, Illinois, April 11, 1981) Copyright by J. Jeffery Auer.

Avery, William T. "Roman Ghost-Writers" (*Classical Journal*, Vol. 54, 1959).

Baeder, Donald L. "Chemical Waste: Fact Versus Perception" (*Vital Speeches of the Day*, June 1, 1980).

Baskin, Otis. "Speech Writing—A Major Public Relations Activity?" (Paper presented at the Annual Meeting of the American Academy of Advertising, Newport, Rhode Island, April, 1974).

Billups, Rufus L. "Black History: Torch for the Future" (*Vital Speeches of the Day*, September 15, 1979).

Bolger, William F. "The Postal Service: Success or Failure?" (*Vital Speeches of the Day*, February 1, 1980).

Bormann, Earnest G. "Ethics of Ghostwritten Speeches" (*Quarterly Journal of Speech*, October, 1961).

————— "Ghostwriting Speeches—A Reply" (*Quarterly Journal of Speech*, December, 1961)

Brigance, William Norwood. *Speech: Its Techniques and Disciplines in a Free Society* (Appleton-Century-Crofts, 2nd ed., 1961).

Buckley, Robert J. "Management Short-Fall in the 1980's: A Threat for the American Economy" (*Vital Speeches of the Day*, February 1, 1980).

Burson-Marsteller. *The Executive Speechmaker: A Systems Approach* (Foundation for Public Relations Research and Education, New York, 1980).

Busse, James G. "Ghostwriters in the Executive Suite" (*TWA Ambassador*, June, 1978).

Butler, Owen "Television Can Show and Tell, But Can It Listen?" (*Vital Speeches of the Day*, August 1, 1981).

Caldwell, John L. "American Purpose and International Human Rights" (*Vital Speeches of the Day*, February 1, 1980).

Capen, Richard G. "Generating Good Signs" (*Vital Speeches of the Day*, October 1, 1980).

Cecil, Andrew R. "Independence and World Citizenship" (*Vital Speeches of the Day*, August 1, 1980).

Chang, Mei-Jung and Gruner, Charles R. "Audience Reaction to Self-Disparaging Humor" (*Southern Speech Communication Journal*, Summer, 1981).

Chisholm, Shirley. "Vote for the Individual, Not the Political Party" (*Vital Speeches of the Day*, August 15, 1978).

181

Costello, John. "Jests Can Do Justice to Your Speeches" (*Nation's Business*, January, 1978).

Cox, LaWanda and John H. "Andrew Johnson and His Ghost Writers: An Analysis of the Freedmen's Bureau and Civil Rights Veto Messages" (*Mississippi Valley Historical Review*, Vol. 48, 1961).

Crutchfield, Edward. "Profitable Banking in the 1980's" (*Vital Speeches of the Day*, June 15, 1980).

Dayton, Kenneth N. "The Case for Corporate Philanthropy" (*Vital Speeches of the Day*, August 1, 1980).

Dee, Robert F. "Musical Glasses and the Milky Way" An address delivered by the CEO of Smithkline Corporation to the Fourth Franklin Conference, November 23, 1979.

Delaney, R. E. "Mick." "The Executive Speech Maker" Also has information on availability of entertaining speakers. Some of Delaney's humorous speeches are available on tape. Box 15259, Wedgewood, Seattle, WA 98115.

Devlin, L. Patrick. "The Influences of Ghostwriting on Rhetorical Criticism" (*Today's Speech*, Number 3, 1974).

Eller, Karl. "Miracle in a Glass: The Free Enterprise System" (*Vital Speeches of the Day*, February 1, 1979).

Ehninger, Douglas, Bruce E. Gronbeck and Alan H. Monroe, *Principles of Speech Communication* (Scott, Foresman and Company, 8th Brief Ed., 1980).

Enos, Richard L. "The Persuasive and Social Force of Logography in Ancient Greece" (*Central States Speech Journal*, Vol. 25, 1974).

Fallows, James. "The Passionless Presidency" (*The Atlantic*, May, 1979 and June 1979).

Fettig, Art. "Humorize Your Speeches" An audio tape. 31 East Avenue South, Battle Creek, MI 49017. Fettig offers a variety of sources of material on speaking and humor.

Fippinger, Grace. "This is a Very Good Time" (*Vital Speeches of the Day*, January 15, 1980).

Freshley, Dwight L. "Gubernatorial Ghost Writers" (*Southern Speech Journal*, Winter, 1965).

Glade, Otto W. "Getting Additional Mileage Out of That Speech" (*Journal of Organizational Communication*, Volume 4, Number 4, 1975).

Golden, James L. "John F. Kennedy and the 'Ghosts'" (*Quarterly Journal of Speech*, Vol. 52, 1966).

Gould, Charles. "Stop Tampering with the Machinery" (*Vital Speeches of the Day*, February 1, 1980).

Grayson, Mel. "Ghosts at the Podium" (*Advertising Age*, October 9, 1978).

Hanley, John. "Lessons I've Learned Since Graduation" (*Vital Speeches of the Day*, July 15, 1981).

————— "Why Ban Reason From the Consumer Safety Debate?" An address before the Town Hall of California, Los Angeles, June 14, 1977.

Honan, William H. "The Men Behind Nixon's Speeches" (*New York Times Magazine*, January 19, 1969).

Huskey, Ken W. *Spokesperson* (K. W. Huskey Associates, 1980). A good book on the skills of public speaking and meeting the press for business speakers. Available from P.O. Box 2715, Palm Springs, CA 92263.

Jebb, R. C. *Attic Orators* (Macmillan and Company, 1876) 2 vols.

Jones, Barrie. "The Understanding of Scale" (*Vital Speeches of the Day*, January 15, 1980).

Kennedy, George. *The Art of Persuasion in Greece* (Princeton University Press, 1963).

Kelley, Joseph J., Jr. *Speechwriting: The Master Touch* (Stackpole Books, 1980).

Kilpatrick, James Jackson. *Richmond News-Leader*, September 12, 1981.

Lichacz, Janine A. "The Art of Corporate Speech Writing: Trends and Techniques" (Master's Thesis, Fairfield University, March, 1980).

Loden, Marilyn. "Networking: It Can Change Your Life" (*Vital Speeches of the Day*, August 1, 1981).

Love, Howard M. "Reindustrialization: Friend or Foe?" (*Vital Speeches of the Day*, January 15, 1981).

Lovell, W. M. "How to Shape A Speech—From Invitation to Podium" (*Journal of Organizational Communication*, 1978, Number 2).

Lynch, Dudley. "It's Time We Give the Brain its Due" (*Journal of Organizational Communication* 1981, Number 1).

Mahoney, David. "National Issues and Consumer Attitudes" (*Vital Speeches of the Day*, July 1, 1978).

May, Ernest R. "Ghost Writing and History" (*The American Scholar*, Vol. 22, 1953).

McDonald, John B. "Rose Garden Rubbish" (*Wall Street Journal*, January 1, 1977).

McGillicuddy, John F. "The Economy, Energy and the President's Proposals" (*Vital Speeches of the Day*, September 15, 1979).

McGinnis, Mack. "Comedy & Comments" Humorous material gathered largely from newspaper columns and distributed by McGinnis twice a month. 448 North Mitchner Avenue, Indianapolis, IN 46219.

McGlon, Charles A. "How I Prepare my Sermons: A Symposium" (*Quarterly Journal of Speech*, February, 1954).

Miller, Casey and Kate Swift. *The Handbook of Nonsexist Writing for Writers, Editors and Speakers* (Lippincott & Crowell, New York, 1980).

Nizer, Louis. *Thinking on Your Feet; Adventures in Speaking.* Garden City, 1944.

Newell, Sara A. and Thomas King. "The Keynote Address of the Democratic National Convention, 1972: The Evolution of a Speech" (*Southern Speech Communication Journal*, Vol. 39, 1974).

Nichols, Marie Hochmuth. *Rhetoric and Criticism* (Louisiana State University Press, 1963). See pp. 35-48 for consideration of the effect of speech writing on academic efforts to evaluate speeches.

Oliver, Robert T. "Syngman Rhee: A Case Study in Transnational Oratory" (*Quarterly Journal of Speech*, Vol. 48, 1962). Describes Oliver's work as Rhee's speech writer.

Ong, John D. "The U. S. Tire Industry in the 1980's" (*Vital Speeches of the*

Day, December 1, 1980).

Orben, Robert. *4 Ways to Improve Your Public Speaking* (The Comedy Center, 1982). Includes "The Care and Heeding of Speechwriters" and "How to Spice Up Those Dull Speeches" Available from the Center, 700 Orange Street, Wilmington, DE 19801).

————— "Orben's Current Comedy" Bi-Monthly. The Comedy Center, 700 Orange Street, Wilmington, DE 19801).

Ott, John. *How to Write And Deliver a Speech* (Cornerstone Library, c1970, 1976).

Pearson, Lester B. "The Four Faces of Peace" Nobel Peace Prize Acceptance Speech, Oslo, Norway, 1957.

Peterson, Peter G. "The Oil and Debt and Poverty Emergence of the Eighties" *(Vital Speeches of the Day,* December 15, 1980).

Persico, Joseph E. "The Rockefeller Rhetoric: Writing Speeches for the 1970 Campaign" *(Today's Speech,* Spring, 1972).

Pickens, Judy E. *Without Bias* (John Wiley & Sons, 1981).

Pope, Jean. "Care and Feeding of Speechwriters" *(Public Relations Journal,* May, 1979).

Poriotis, Wesley. "Is There Life After Manuscript?" *(Public Relations Journal,* July, 1981).

Postman, Neil. "The Technical Thesis" *(Vital Speeches of the Day,* January 1, 1979).

Potter, Norman D. "Leadership: The Need for Renaissance" *(Vital Speeches of the Day,* January 1, 1980).

Reichardt, Carl E. "Does Two Plus Two Equal Five?" *(Vital Speeches of Day,* September 15, 1981).

Reagan, Ronald. "Inaugural Address" *(Vital Speeches of the Day,* February 15, 1981).

Rockefeller, David. "The Chief Executive in the Year 2000" *(Vital Speeches of the Day,* January 1, 1980).

Rosenman, Samuel I. *Working with Roosevelt* (Harper and Brothers, New York, 1952).

Safire, William. *Before the Fall* (Tower Publications, 1975).

————— "Reagan Betrays A Lack of Homework" *(Richmond Times-Dispatch,* June 19, 1981).

Shapiro, Irving. "The Lawyer's Special Role" *(Vital Speeches of the Day,* February 15, 1979).

Shrum, Robert. "No Private Smiles" *(New Times,* June 11, 1976).

Smith, Craig R. "Appendum to 'Contemporary Political Speech Writing'" *(Southern Speech Communication Journal,* Winter, 1977).

————— "Contemporary Political Speech Writing." *(Southern Speech Communication Journal,* Fall, 1976).

Smith, Donald K. "Ghostwritten Speeches" *(Quarterly Journal of Speech,* December 1961).

Sorensen, Theodore C. *Decision-Making in the White House* (Columbia University Press, New York, 1963).

Staley, D. C. "Can We Get There from Here?" *(Vital Speeches of the Day,*

November 1, 1980).

Teresa, Mother. "The Gift of Peace" (*Vital Speeches of the Day*, June 1, 1980).

Toot, Joseph F. "The Lost and Crucial Art" (*Vital Speeches of the Day*, February 1, 1980).

Tower, Raymond C. "Government Regulation: Slow Death for Free Enterprise" (*Vital Speeches of the Day*, September 1, 1980).

Usher, S. "Lysias and His Clients" (*Greek, Roman, and Byzantine Studies*, Vol. 17, 1976).

Van Andel, Jay. "Business Leadership Against Inflation" (*Vital Speeches of the Day*, July 1, 1979).

Wise, Paul S. "The Arson for Profit Business" (*Vital Speeches of the Day*, November 1, 1978).

Woolsey, R. James. "Decision Making in Designing U.S. Naval Forces" (*Vital Speeches of the Day*, July 1, 1978).

NOTES

Vital Speeches of the Day can be found in almost any library. It is published twice monthly by the City News Publishing Company, Box 606, Southold, NY 11971.

Management consultants who specialize in the market for speech writers include Jean Cardwell, Cardwell Consultants, Box 59418, Chicago, IL 60659; Bill Cantor, The Cantor Concern, 39 West 59th Street, New York, NY 10019; Larry Marshall, Marshall Consultants, Inc., 360 East 65th Street, New York, NY 10021; and Wesley Poriotis, Wesley-Brown Enterprises, 745 Fifth Avenue, Suite 1516, New York, NY 10022.

Newsletters published for speech writers are *Speechwriter's Newsletter*, Ragan Communications, 407 South Dearborn, Chicago, IL 60605, and *The Effective Speech Writer's Newsletter*, The Effective Speech Writing Institute, P.O. Box 444, University of Richmond, VA 23173.

INDEX